English Writing for Academic Purposes

A Course Book for Graduate Students of Science and Technology

研究生学术英语写作

理工类

总主编　陈新仁　黄　燕

主　编　刘应亮　郑景婷

副主编　奚　洁

编　者　刘应亮　郑景婷
　　　　奚　洁　徐　娟

清华大学出版社
北京

内 容 简 介

《研究生学术英语写作：理工类》是"研究生学术英语实用教程"系列教材之一。本教材面向研究生学术英语论文写作的现实需求，细致呈现学术英语体裁，尤其是理工类学术论文的结构特征和语言特点，旨在锻炼研究生学术英语写作能力。与同类教材相比，本教材更具系统性和操作性，学科覆盖面广，支持研究型学习，可以满足研究生和高年级本科生快速有效提升学术写作能力的需求。

本教材另配有练习的答案详解，读者可登录 ftp://ftp.tup.tsinghua.edu.cn/ 下载使用。

版权所有，侵权必究。举报：010-62782989，beiqinquan@tup.tsinghua.edu.cn。

图书在版编目（CIP）数据

研究生学术英语写作：理工类 / 陈新仁，黄燕总主编；刘应亮，郑景婷主编 . —北京：清华大学出版社，2022.8（2024.2重印）
ISBN 978-7-302-60919-3

Ⅰ.①研… Ⅱ.①陈… ②黄… ③刘… ④郑… Ⅲ.①英语—论文—写作—研究生—教学参考资料 Ⅳ.① H319.36

中国版本图书馆 CIP 数据核字（2022）第 088660 号

责任编辑：方燕贝　刘　艳
封面设计：李尘工作室
责任校对：王凤芝
责任印制：曹婉颖

出版发行：清华大学出版社
　　　网　　址：https://www.tup.com.cn，https://www.wqxuetang.com
　　　地　　址：北京清华大学学研大厦A座　　邮　编：100084
　　　社 总 机：010-83470000　　邮　购：010-62786544
　　　投稿与读者服务：010-62776969，c-service@tup.tsinghua.edu.cn
　　　质量反馈：010-62772015，zhiliang@tup.tsinghua.edu.cn
印 装 者：大厂回族自治县彩虹印刷有限公司
经　　销：全国新华书店
开　　本：185mm×260mm　　印　张：13.5　　字　数：260 千字
版　　次：2022 年 9 月第 1 版　　　　　　　印　次：2024 年 2 月第 2 次印刷
定　　价：59.00 元

产品编号：095242-01

总　序

研究生教育肩负着国家高层次人才培养和创新创造的重要使命，是国家发展、社会进步的重要基石。研究生英语课程对于持续提高研究生的人文素养和专业能力，培养学生的家国情怀和创新精神，引导学生坚定文化自信、学术自信，成为有理想、有国际学术视野的高层次、创新性人才，从而更好地服务于国家的发展战略，都具有不可替代的重要作用。

为贯彻落实教育部印发的《高等学校课程思政建设指导纲要》，彰显立德树人根本宗旨，培养研究生的学术英语能力和跨文化交流能力，深入推进新时代研究生培养国际化，我们秉持以学生学习为中心的教育学理念，结合我国研究生英语学习实际需求和教学现状，策划编写了本套"研究生学术英语实用教程"系列教材，由《研究生学术英语阅读：理工类》《研究生学术英语阅读：人文类》《研究生学术英语写作：理工类》《研究生学术英语写作：人文类》《研究生学术英语视听说》共五册教材构成。

本套教材的编写原则与思路如下：

一、以立德树人为总目标，秉承以学生发展为中心、以学生学习为中心的理念，两个中心相辅相成，互为支撑。以学生发展为中心体现在将思政教育有机融入教材设计中，内容选择与问题设计体现中国学术贡献、学术诚信、文化自信、科学素养等思政元素。以学生学习为中心体现在内容设计围绕真实的学术活动展开，满足学生用英语进行专业学习、开展国际学术交流的现实需要。

二、着眼于跨文化学术交际，体现国际化人才培养的定位。本套教材将学术交流置于跨文化语境之中，注重培养学生的国际视野和跨文化学术交际意识，提升跨文化沟通中所需的学术交流能力和思辨能力。一方面，各分册的选材都能兼顾中外学者、中英文学术语篇，提供比较分析的机会。另一方面，各分册所选语料都蕴含具体的学术体裁知识，为学生习得跨文化学术交流所需的各种学术英语知识提供必要的支持。

三、本着"在用中学"的编写理念，着力于学生多元能力培养。新时代深化研究生培养改革，必须着力增强研究生实践能力、创新能力等多元能力的培养。本套教材强调能力培养至上而非知识传授至上。各分册采用"以项目为导向"的学术英语教学方法，注重实际学术活动的参与和体验，以输入驱动输出，将听、说、读、写、译五项语言技能有机融合，强调综合语言应用能力、合作学习、自主学习能力的培养，激励学生通过讨论及修改反例等练习形式提升批判性思辨能力。

四、体现学术共性与学科差异。基于大类学科（如理工类、人文类）的特点，设计各分册，每个分册选材真实地道，来源多样，内涵丰富。同一单元涵盖多门学科，体现大学科特色，以支撑高校主流学科国际化人才的培养。

五、体现信息技术支撑。为实现教材编写目标，培养学生的自主学习能力，本套教材在各分册中都设计了让学生利用互联网自主查找文献或相关资源的教学活动。另外，全套教材采用线上与线下相结合的方式提供课堂教学资源和拓展学习资源。

本着上述编写原则和思路，"研究生学术英语实用教程"系列教材形成以下鲜明特色：

- **育人性**。各分册每个单元都有课程思政的元素，全套教材强调学术诚信和科学素养，力求将育人寓于学术英语知识传授和多元能力培养之中。

- **实用性**。全套教材所选语料来源于真实学术活动，内容设计贴近学生实际阅读、写作、听说需求，为其英语学习提供全面、切实、有效的指导。

- **针对性**。全套教材面向国内非英语专业研究生，在整个编写过程中，以学生为中心，关注他们的实际需求，聚焦他们在学习过程中的重难点，力求合理把握教学内容的难度，为学生提供丰富的、可学可用的语料。

- **可操作性**。全套教材练习形式多样，采用结对练习、小组讨论等形式凸显互动性和合作性，强调获得感。各分册均由八个单元构成，可满足 16 个标准课堂学时的教学需要，服务课堂操作。

作为体现学术共性与学科差异的学术英语系列教材，本套教材可以满足不同院校、不同学科研究生英语教学的需要。我们诚挚欢迎广大英语教师和各位学生在使用本套教材的过程中，能以各种方式提供反馈意见和建议，以便我们不断完善，打造一套启智润心、增知强能的系列精品教材！

陈新仁、黄燕
2022 年 4 月

前　言

《研究生学术英语写作：理工类》是"研究生学术英语实用教程"系列教材之一。在具体呈现整套教材立德树人的总体编写理念、思路与特色的基础上，本教材旨在指导我国理工科研究生撰写英语学术论文，聚力训练他们的学术写作表达能力，特别是撰写国际期刊论文的实际能力。

本册特色

一、英语学术论文全流程覆盖。本教材的内容编排以英语学术论文的一般流程为依据，指导学生掌握撰写英语学术论文各个部分所需的组织技巧和语言策略，提升学生的学术英语写作能力。

二、英语写作技能训练全方位融合。本教材针对学生在研究生阶段提升学术英语写作能力的需求，将理论讲解、案例分析、专项技能训练和团队任务训练深度结合，帮助学生全面提升学术交流场景下的语言应用能力。

教材构成

本教材以学术写作为主线，根据英语论文的各个部分和撰写进程进行内容编排，共设八个单元。每个单元针对英语论文的具体部分展开，主题依次为标题和摘要、引言、研究方法、结果和讨论、结论、综述类文章、对评审意见的回复以及作者简介。

每个单元的主体内容包括四个板块。Part Ⅰ Introducing the Unit 为内容概览，旨在帮助学生了解教学目标，并快速获取单元主要内容。Part Ⅱ Learning Useful Expressions 列举学术写作常用句型，为学生提供具有不同功能的核心词汇和丰富句型，不仅方便学生记忆、操练，还为后续的任务训练做好准备。Part Ⅲ Learning Ways of Organization 介绍篇章结构，结合相关理论和研究，讲解本单元论文相关部分的语言特点和篇章组织方式。Part Ⅳ Analyzing the Examples 是案例分析，通过对国际期刊论文的节选内容进行分析，帮助学生深入了解单元内容。之后还设有 Exercises 和 Project 两个板块。前者设计形式多样的练习（补全信息、填空、翻译、排序、简答等），着重训练学生撰写论文不同部分的写作技能；材料选自不同理工学科国际知名期刊，遵循难度递进的原则。后者是团队项目，要求学生利用所学写作技能解决实际问题，并做课堂汇报。

为保持真实性，教材所选语料在维持原样的基础上修改了少数语法错误和不恰当用法。同时，为尊重当事人隐私，编辑和审稿人与作者往来信件和材料中涉及个人隐私的姓名、期刊名称、收稿编号等信息均作了匿名处理。

教学建议

每个单元的六个板块组成一个有机的整体。Part Ⅰ、Part Ⅱ 和 Part Ⅲ 为课前阅读内容，要求学生课前进行预习，教师可在课堂上检查学生的掌握情况并适当补充讲解；Part Ⅳ 和 Exercises 板块为课堂操练内容，教师可采用小组讨论等各种互动形式，让学生进行全面、有效的练习，并在课堂上及时提供反馈建议；Project 板块要求学生自主查询论文并做分析，教师可以布置为课后小组作业，要求学生在下次课上进行小组汇报。建议每四个课时教授一个单元，教师也可以根据具体情况灵活处理和安排。

编写分工

本教材由刘应亮、郑景婷担任主编，奚洁担任副主编，徐娟参与编写。各单元分工情况如下：刘应亮负责第三、第四单元；郑景婷负责第五、第七单元；奚洁负责第一、第八单元；徐娟负责第二、第六单元。陈新仁教授和黄燕教授作为总主编，负责审阅、修改和润色文稿。

由于编者水平有限，书中难免存在疏漏和错误之处，敬请广大同仁和英语学习者不吝批评指正。

编者

2022 年 5 月

Contents

Unit 1 **Titles and Abstracts** ·· 1

Unit 2 **Introductions** ·· 25

Unit 3 **Methodological Descriptions** ··· 53

Unit 4 **Results and Discussions** ·· 75

Unit 5 **Conclusions** ·· 93

Unit 6 **Review Articles** ·· 111

Unit 7 **Responses to Reviewers' Comments and Editors' Decisions** ·· 139

Unit 8 **Bio-notes and CVs** ·· 167

References ··· 199

Unit 1

Titles and Abstracts

Part I
Introducing the Unit

A suitable title and an appropriate abstract give the "initial impressions" of a paper. For this reason, they need to be drafted correctly, accurately, carefully, and meticulously. They are often drafted after the whole manuscript is completed.

The title and the abstract are the most visible parts of an academic article. During peer review, invited reviewers are asked to decide whether they wish to review the manuscript on the basis of the title and the abstract alone. When the article is published, on many occasions more people will read the title and the abstract than the whole article. Or, many people will only read the title and the abstract before they decide whether they want to move on. It is thus important to attract readers' attention by making the title and the abstract as concise, accurate, and readable as possible.

In today's academic research, most people rely on electronic search engines to search through databases (for example in the medical science MEDLINE and PubMed) which only include titles, author lists, and abstracts of articles. Therefore, it is important to draft the title and/or the abstract in a way that they are most likely to attract scholars.

In this unit, by reading, analyzing, and comparing the titles and abstracts of some research articles from renowned academic journals in science and technology, we will learn how to write proper titles and abstracts, in terms of wording and style, as well as moves in the abstracts.

After finishing this unit, you are expected to achieve the following learning objectives:

- to understand the purposes and significance of writing effective titles and abstracts of academic papers;
- to understand the structures and styles of titles and abstracts in different fields of natural sciences;
- to use phrases and sentence templates effectively in writing titles and abstracts.

Unit 1   Titles and Abstracts

Part II
Learning Useful Expressions

Study the bold-faced expressions that are often used in the titles and abstracts of journal articles.

Useful Expressions for Titles

A. Stating the Purpose, Topic, or Findings of the Research

- A Global Perspective on Local Meteoric Water Lines: **Meta-analytic Insight into** Fundamental Controls and Practical Constraints
- **A** Modified Backward Elimination **Approach for** the Rapid Classification of Chinese Ceramics Using Laser-Induced Breakdown Spectroscopy and Chemometrics
- Abrupt Emissions Reductions During COVID-19 **Contributed to** Record Summer Rainfall in China
- CDBV: **A** Driving **Dataset** with Chinese Characteristics **from a** Bike **View**
- **Development and Validation of** a New Algorithm for Attribution of Neuropsychiatric Events in Systemic Lupus Erythematosus
- **On Solving** Ambiguity Resolution with Robust Chinese Remainder Theorem for Multiple Numbers
- **On Standardization of** Basic Datasets of Electronic Medical Records in Traditional Chinese Medicine
- One Hundred Days of Coronavirus Disease 2019 **Prevention and Control** in China
- Population Density and **Driving Factors of** North China Leopards in Tieqiaoshan Nature Reserve
- **Real-time Forecasting and Early Warning of** Bacillary Dysentery Activity in Four Meteorological and Geographic Divisions in China

B. Indicating the Types of the Research

- **Using** a Smartphone Camera **to Explore** Ray Optics Beyond the Thin Lens Equation
- **Strategies for** Synthesis of 1,3,4-Oxadiazole Derivatives and Their Biological

Activities: **A Mini Review**

- **A Review of** Physics Simulators for Robotic Applications
- **A Theoretical Analysis of** Deep Q-learning
- **Correspondence to** Proton Pump Inhibitors and Risk of Colorectal Cancer
- **Commentary on** the Mathematical Model of the Human Circadian System by Kronauer et al.
- **A Prospective Study of** Cannabis Use as a Risk Factor for Non-adherence and Treatment Dropout in First-episode Schizophrenia
- **A Randomized Clinical Trial** Investigating the Efficacy of Targeted Nutrition as Adjunct to Exercise Training in COPD
- **An Empirical Evaluation of** Generic Convolutional and Recurrent Networks for Sequence Modeling
- **An Observational Study of** the Evolution of Horizontal Convective Rolls
- Genetic Mutations in Plants: **A Comparative Study of** How Climate Changes and the Contemporary Urban Lifestyle Have Led to the Change in the Scenery of Flora in the Different Ecosystems

C. Providing the Methods and Study Design in the Research

- **A Multivariate Analysis of** 416 Patients with Glioblastoma Multiforme: Prognosis, Extent of Resection, and Survival
- **A Qualitative Study on** the Psychological Experience of Caregivers of COVID-19 Patients
- Association of E-cigarette Use with Oral Health: **A Population-based Cross-sectional Questionnaire Study**
- Equine-facilitated Learning for Youths with Severe Emotional Disorders: **A Quantitative and Qualitative Study**
- Exploring University Students' Preferences for Educational Robot Design by Means of **a User-centered Design Approach**
- Meeting an 80% Reduction in Greenhouse Gas Emissions from Transportation by 2050: **A Case Study in** California
- Nurses on the Move: **A Quantitative Report on** How Meditation Can Improve Nurse Performance
- Paracetamol: Not as Safe as We Thought? **A Systematic Literature Review of**

Observational Studies

Useful Expressions for Abstracts

A. Introducing the Background or Significance of the Study

- Among them, Nonnegative Matrix Factorization (NMF) **has received considerable attention** due to its psychological and physiological interpretation of naturally occurring data whose representation may be parts based in the human brain.
- However, our ability to detect BD dynamics and outbreaks **remains limited** in China.
- Structural visualization and analysis **are fundamental to** explore macromolecular functions.
- Studies to determine mechanisms underlying the metabolic decompensation in minority populations with a history of hyperglycemic crises **are a major area of interest within the field of** diabetes.
- The increase in stream length ratio from lower to higher order shows that **the study area has reached a** mature geomorphic **stage**.
- The North China leopard is a subspecies of leopard distributed in China, **but little is known about** its population status.
- With the rising concerns about algorithmic bias, **a growing body of literature has attempted to** understand and resolve the issue of algorithmic bias.

B. Leading to the Research Question or Research Objectives

- **In this paper we consider** the classification of closed non-collapsed ancient solutions to the Mean Curvature Flow ($n \geqslant 2$) that are uniformly two-convex.
- **The current research is an effort towards** the standardization of basic dataset of electronic medical records in traditional Chinese medicine.
- **The purpose of this investigation was to explore** an alternative field test to estimate maximal oxygen consumption using a one-mile walk test.
- **This study attempts to determine** the effectiveness, efficiency, and cost of chiropractic treatment for patients with low back pain.
- **This study selected** the most active areas of North China leopards **to determine** the population density and distribution of North China leopards.
- **This study aims to systematically review and analyze** the available

literature on "exceptional responders" in oncology.
- **This study introduces the notion of** a complex cell, a complexification of the cells/cylinders used in real-time geometry.

C. Briefing the Study Design or Research Methods

- **A retrospective analysis of** 24 MPNST patients, treated from 1994 to 2002, in the department of Surgical Oncology at All India Institute of Medical Sciences, New Delhi, was done.
- In this study, we **conducted** camera-trap **surveys of** a North China Leopard population in Tieqiaoshan Nature Reserve, Shanxi Province, China.
- In this work, **an** outpatient clinical information **model** and an inpatient clinical information model **are created to** adequately depict the diagnosis processes and treatment procedures of traditional Chinese medicine.
- Therefore, **an empirical approach was taken to investigate/explore the relationship between** proportional reporting ratios (PRRs) and relative risk (RR) estimates from formal studies in a set of known adverse drug reactions (ADRs).
- We **conducted a** phase 3, double-blind, randomized, placebo-controlled discontinuation **trial involving** patients with psychosis related to Alzheimer's disease, Parkinson's disease, and dementia.
- We **conducted a systematic literature review** to assess the adverse event (AE) profile of paracetamol.
- We **used a test-negative case-control design to estimate** the efficacy of vaccination against symptomatic disease caused by the delta variant.

D. Reporting the Findings or Stating the Conclusion

- **A positive effect of** temperature **was observed** when weekly mean temperature exceeded 4 ℃, –3 ℃, 9 ℃, and 16 ℃ in Beijing (Northern China), Shenyang (Northeast China), Chongqing (Southwest China), and Shenzhen (Southern China), respectively.
- However, given the wide confidence intervals for the estimate of effect, the findings do not **allow for a conclusive interpretation.**
- **Of four studies reporting** renal AEs, **three reported** a dose-response with one reporting an increasing OR of ⩾ 30% decrease in estimated glomerular filtration rate from 1.40 (0.79 to 2.48) to 2.19 (1.4 to 3.43).
- Postoperative radiotherapy (RT) **has shown a definite role in** both disease

Unit 1　Titles and Abstracts

free and overall survival in this study.
- **The outcome of this research** is a proposal of standardized traditional Chinese medicine medical records datasets.
- **The results could suggest that** quasiparticle decoherence extends to dopings well beyond the pseudogap regime.
- **The results demonstrate that** the proposed algorithm is more efficient in reducing the redundant features and computational time and improve the model performance.
- **These insights informed us that** in order to protect this predator, which is only distributed in China, we should adopt a comprehensive, customized, adaptive landscape protection strategy.

Part III
Learning Ways of Organization

In this part, we are going to discuss the structures of titles and abstracts so as to develop the skills of writing titles and abstracts of academic papers in science and technology.

Writing Appropriate Titles for Articles

The title is of paramount importance for an article because a reader first looks at the title of the article to decide its relevancy to his or her academic interest.

In terms of the functions of titles, there are three most common formats:

- descriptive titles: describing the subject of the article but withholding the main conclusions (e.g., "The Effects of Family Support on Patients with Dementia; Complex Cellular Structures");
- declarative titles: stating the main findings or conclusions (e.g., "A Statin a Day Keeps the Doctor Away: Comparative Proverb Assessment Modeling Study");
- interrogative titles: introducing the subject in the form of a question (e.g., "Are There Rearrangement Hotspots in the Human Genome?").

In academic journal articles of natural sciences, titles are classified into five categories according to their structures. They are:

- nominal phrase titles: consisting of one short phrase or more than one which encapsulates the theme of the article (e.g., "The Hallmark of Cancer; Magnetic Field in the Intergalactic Region");
- compound nominal phrase titles: comprising two phrases in succession, in which the initial phrase is the main title of the article, and the second phrase, usually following a colon or a dash mark, serves to further delimit the theme of the paper or to state the methods of the research (e.g., "Analysis of Serum 10 years Prior to 1st Diagnosis of Hepatitis C Related Hepatocellular Carcinoma: A Case-control Study"; "Krabbe Disease: Clinical Profile"; "Markov Chain Importance Sampling: A Highly Efficient Estimator for MCMC");
- verbal phrase titles: initiated by a verb, whether in to-infinite form or in present participle form (e.g., "To See, Or Not to See? Rifted Margin Extension"; "Identifying and Tracking SARS-CoV-2 Variants: A Challenge and an Opportunity");
- prepositional titles: initiated by a preposition (e.g., "From Collections of Independent, Mindless Robots to Flexible, Mobile, and Directional Superstructures");
- full-sentence titles: containing a statement or a question, which are rare but often deemed less ambiguous than a nominal or compound title (e.g., "Zircon-Modeled Melts Shed Light on the Formation of Earth's Crust from the Hadean to the Archean"; "How Effective Are the Various Types of Medication in Treating Elementary Studies with ADHD?").

To write an effective title for a journal article, the author can follow the following tips. Firstly, an informative, specific, accurate title should include essential scientific "keywords" for indexing so as to help the reader predict the content of the research paper. Secondly, the author should avoid using abbreviations and writing scientific names in full, e.g., "Escherichia coli" rather than "E. coli"; "Ca" for calcium could be mistaken for "CA", which means cancer. Thirdly, to get the paper published successfully, the author should adhere to the word count and other instructions as specified by the target journal. In addition, he or she should refer to the specific journals and the styles (e.g., the AMA style in the bioethics sciences and the AIP style in physics and astronomy) for more information about the capitalization style and general form of article titles. In writing an academic journal article, the author should follow the right style of capitalization and be consistent. Usually, there are three capitalization styles in titles: capitalizing the first letter of the beginning word in the title, capitalizing the first letter of each content word and the first letter of each function word of more than four letters, and capitalizing every letter in the title.

> Writing Effective Abstracts for Academic Conferences and Journal Articles

The abstract is a summary or synopsis of the entire research paper and also needs to have similar characteristics like the title. It must outline the most important aspects of the study and highlight the selling points of the manuscript so as to lure the reader to read the whole paper.

A conference abstract is a brief summary of the paper a scholar wants to present at an academic conference. Submitting research work to a conference is a primary way to get one's work disseminated, and to create opportunities and collaborative network with researchers in the relevant academic fields. The scholar has to do some research to learn about the topic of the conference so as to tailor the abstract to fit specific sessions. The scholar has to check all the requirements, including formatting, word limits, submission deadline, etc. of the conference organizer. The word limits for most conference abstracts are around 250~300 words, or even less. Today, scholars usually submit conference abstracts electronically and attach any supporting documents that may be required by the organizers.

In the natural and applied sciences, the abstract format varies depending on the discipline and the journal. Some journals, like *Cell* and *Nature*, prefer unstructured (or non-structured) abstracts, a single paragraph to summarize the key points of the manuscript. Unstructured abstracts are free-flowing, do not have predefined subheadings, and are commonly used for papers that usually do not describe original research. Also, many journal articles follow the standard IMRaD format (an acronym for Introduction, Methods, Results, and Discussion, the format for the sections of a research report), using the four-point structured abstracts, such as *The New England Journal of Medicine*. In IMRaD format, under each subheading the authors compose the essential information of the research. A structured abstract is more elaborate, informative, easy to read, recall, and peer-review, and hence is preferred in some disciplines such as the bioethics sciences. Both formats of abstracts include four basic moves, the discourse or rhetorical units that perform a coherent communicative function in written or spoken discourse. In IMRaD format, the four moves are usually labeled with the following subheadings, although these moves are not marked in the one-paragraph abstract.

Here are the four moves in abstract writing:

- Introduction/Background/Objectives: Under this subheading, authors state the rationale of the research, the hypothesis, or the major objectives.
- Methods: This section states what was done, and gives essential details of the study design, setting, participants, sample size and method, intervention(s), duration and follow-up, research instruments, main outcome measures, parameters evaluated, and how the outcomes were assessed or analyzed.
- Results: This section reports the main findings with data and concisely describes how the results pertain to the study aim or hypothesis. This section is usually the longest one of the four moves.
- Conclusion: This section is usually composed of one or two sentences that help the reader understand the results and implications of the research. This part discusses whether the hypothesis was correct and whether the original purpose was achieved. This section also summarizes significant theoretical or practical implications the research may have and recommends further research, if necessary.

In the following abstract of "Neoarchean Basement, Mantle Enrichment and Crustal Extraction in Central Asia: Petrogenesis of 2.5 Ga Amphibolite and Metadiorite in NE China" (Liu et al., 2021), an article from *American Journal of Science*, we can see how the move structure is applied in the one-paragraph abstract.

> Archean basement in the Central Asian Orogenic Belt (CAOB) is relatively rare, but it has the potential to provide additional information on the processes of lithospheric mantle enrichment and crust extraction processes during the early history of the Earth. We identified Neoarchean amphibolite (2537–2565 Ma) and metadiorite (2481–2539 Ma) in the Biliya area of the Erguna Terrane in the southeast CAOB. The amphibolite is geochemically MORB-like and has a weakly left-leaning REE pattern, and low zircon $\varepsilon Hf(t)$ (−0.7– +6.2), and whole-rock $\varepsilon Nd(t)$ (−1.7– +4.5) and $\varepsilon Hf(t)$ (−1.9) values. Our petrogenetic modeling reveals that the amphibolite is derived from ~20% partial melting of the lithospheric mantle in

> the spinel stability field (~65 km depth). The metadiorite shows near-zero εNd(t) (−0.5– +3.6) and εHf(t) (+0.5– +1.4) values and is likely derived from partial melting of mafic lower crust. The metadiorite and amphibolite likely formed in an extensional continental arc/back-arc setting and represent the Archean crystalline basement of the microcontinents within the CAOB. Three-staged mantle segregation and crust extraction processes have been proposed: (1) 20% melt extraction from primitive mantle-like lithospheric mantle, leaving behind a depleted mantle; (2) subduction-related fluid/melt metasomatism of the lithospheric mantle and its partial melting, generating the arc-type enriched mantle and mafic lower crust; and (3) partial remelting of the mafic lower crust produced the Tonalite-trondhjemite-granodiorite (TTG) crust.

This one-paragraph abstract introduces the background and significance of the research, stating that "Archean basement in the Central Asian Orogenic Belt (CAOB) is relatively rare, but it has the potential to provide additional information on the processes of lithospheric mantle enrichment and crust extraction processes during the early history of the Earth". Here the expressions "…is relatively rare" and "…has the potential to…" claim the value of the research. In the following sentences, the authors describe the research procedures about how they "identified" rocks and how they established "petrogenetic modeling" to analyze the formation. In the moves of "Results" and "Conclusion", the "three-staged mantle segregation and crust extraction processes have been proposed" to help understand the results of this research.

The following abstract of biological sciences is different from the one above in that it adopts the structured format.

> **Background and Objectives:** Production of good quality biocatalysts is one important step in optimizing the utilization of agricultural by-products in the development of the Simantri-pattern livestock business. This study has been carried out to evaluate the quality and effectivity of biocatalyst formulated by probiotic lignocellulolytic bacteria from Bali cattle rumen content and termites as the starter of agricultural by-products.
>
> **Materials and Methods:** The five probiotic lignocellulolytic bacteria, namely Bacillus subtilis strain BR$_4$LG, Bacillus subtilis strain BR$_2$CL, Aneurinibacillus sp., strain

BT$_4$LS, Bacillus sp., strain BT$_3$CL, and Bacillus sp., strain BT$_8$XY use for production 10 biocatalyst formula namely B$_0$, B$_1$, B$_2$, B$_3$, B$_4$, B$_5$, B$_{1234}$, B$_{1235}$, B$_{1245}$, and B$_{12345}$ as treatments and six replicated. The biocatalyst quality was evaluated by nutrient contents, bacteria population, and lignocellulose activities. The effectivity of biocatalyst was evaluated by silage nutrient contents, metabolic product (totally VFA and NH3-N), dry matter and organic matter in vitro digestibility of rice straw silage. Analysis of variance (ANOVA) was used to analyze data and followed by Honestly of Significant Difference (HSD) analysis if there are significant differences between treatments.

Results: The utilization of probiotic lignocellulolytic bacteria was able to improve the quality and effectivity of solid biocatalysts produced shown by increasing bacteria, nutrient content, and lignocellulose activity of biocatalyst produce. These biocatalysts increase the quality of nutrient contents, metabolite product, and dry matter and organic matter in vitro digestibility of rice straw silage.

Conclusion: Biocatalyst B$_{12345}$ is the best biocatalyst formula which has the highest quality and effectiveness compared to other biocatalysts.

(Adapted from "Effectivity of Biocatalyst of Probiotic Lignocellulolytic Bacteria as Starter of Agricultural By-product" by I. M. Mudita et al. in *Journal of Biological Sciences*, *22*, 2022.)

The four-point structured abstract is easier to follow with subheadings summarizing the information in each move. In the first move, the authors use expressions such as "…is one important step" and "this study has been carried out to evaluate…" to state the research significance and objectives. In the second move, such sentences as "Analysis of variance (ANOVA) was used to analyze data and followed by Honestly of Significant Difference (HSD) analysis if there are significant differences between treatments" clarify the research methods, including the treatment, the analysis of data, etc. After summarizing the results in the third move, an affirmative statement in the conclusion part helps the reader understand the results better.

Comparing the two examples above, we can see that the choice of the abstract format should depend on the style of a particular journal and therefore is not left to the author's wish. While drafting the abstract, the author should avoid lengthy background information, too many details about routine laboratory procedures, and undefined abbreviations or acronyms. One thing the author has to bear in mind is not to overstate the contribution of the study in the abstract so as not to mislead the readers. Usually, the present tense is used to introduce the study, explain the significance of the study, and justify the rationale for the research, while the past tense is used to describe the previous studies, the research methods, and major research findings.

To sum up, the title and the abstract give the readers the initial impressions of a research article, so they need to:

- include keywords about the research;
- be concise, informative, and precise;
- be often drafted after the complete draft is ready;
- adhere to the instructions laid by the target journal regarding the style and the number of words permitted for the title and the abstract.

Part IV Analyzing the Examples

In this part, we are going to analyze some examples so as to understand the wording, structures, and moves of titles and abstracts of academic papers in science and technology.

I. **Analyze the following titles of research papers and discuss the questions with a partner.**

(1) Population Density and Driving Factors of North China Leopards in Tieqiaoshan Nature Reserve

(2) Probing Earth's Mysterious Inner Core, and the Most Complete Human Genome to Date

(3) Trips and Neurotransmitters: Discovering Principled Patterns Across 6,850 Hallucinogenic Experiences

(4) Cannabidiol Inhibits SARS-CoV-2 Replication Through Induction of the

Host ER Stress and Innate Immune Responses

(5) Direct Observation of Requests for Clinical Services in Office Practice: What Do Patients Want and Do They Get It?

 Questions:

1. What information is given in each title?
2. What type of titles does each title belong to?
3. What structure does each title follow?

II. **Analyze the following titles of research papers and discuss the questions with a partner.**

(1) A Study of Isolated Infective Endocarditis of the Pulmonary Valve: An Autopsy Analysis of Nine Cases

(2) How to Achieve Quantum Annealing via Path-integral Monte Carlo with Data Augmentation

(3) Randomized Trial of Fetal Surgery Causes Severe Left Diaphragmatic Hernia

(4) Data Science and Physical Organic Chemistry

(5) Mortality from Gastrointestinal Congenital Anomalies: An International Study

 Questions:

1. What problems might be with these titles?
2. How would you improve these titles?
3. Why do you improve these titles in that way?

III. **Compare the following three abstracts. What formats do they adopt? What moves do they include? What are the similarities and differences among them?**

Abstract 1

目的：研究 PI3K 抑制剂联合地塞米松对 H_2O_2-TNF α-U937 细胞模型激素敏感性的影

响及其作用机制。

方法：采用过氧化氢（H_2O_2）刺激巨噬细胞系 U937，建立 H_2O_2-TNF α-U937 细胞氧化应激－激素耐受模型（简称"H_2O_2-TNF α-U937 细胞模型"），将磷酸肌醇 3 激酶（PI3K）抑制剂（BEZ235 或 LY294002）单独或联合地塞米松（Dex）干预该模型。使用 PCR 与 ELISA 方法比较其抑制 IL-8 基因与蛋白质的表达水平，组蛋白去乙酰化酶（HDAC）-2 试剂盒检测 HDAC2 活力改变，并通过 Western blot 检测 AP-1、NF-κB 磷酸化水平。

结果：在 H_2O_2-TNF α-U937 细胞模型中，Dex 抑制该细胞模型释放 IL-8 的能力降低，并且单用 PI3K 抑制剂（BEZ235 或 LY294002）不能明显抑制 IL-8 释放（$p < 0.05$），而经 PI3K 抑制剂（BEZ235 或 LY294002）联合 Dex 干预后，细胞对激素的抵抗得到明显改善（$p < 0.05$）。BEZ235 而不是 LY294002 部分逆转了细胞核蛋白 HDAC2 的活力，但两种抑制剂均能相应降低炎症转录因子 NF- B、AP-1 的磷酸化水平。

结论：PI3K 抑制剂联合 Dex 能改善氧化应激诱导的 U937 细胞对激素不敏感性，其机制可能与 PI3K 抑制剂能部分恢复因氧化应激作用导致的 HADC2 活力和降低 NF-κB、AP-1 蛋白磷酸化水平有关。

［关键词］激素不敏感；氧化应激；HDAC2；PI3K 抑制剂

（选自"PI3K 抑制剂联合地塞米松改善氧化应激细胞模型对激素的敏感性及其分子机制"，曾瑜真等，《中国免疫学杂志》，第 37 卷，第 12 期，2022 年）

Abstract 2

Background

Primary cytomegalovirus (CMV) infection during pregnancy carries a risk of congenital infection and possible severe sequelae. There is no established intervention for preventing congenital CMV infection.

Methods

In this multicenter, double-blind trial, pregnant women with primary CMV infection diagnosed before 24 weeks' gestation were randomly assigned to receive a monthly infusion of CMV hyperimmune globulin (at a dose of 100 mg per kilogram of body weight) or matching placebo until delivery. The primary outcome was a composite of congenital CMV infection or fetal or neonatal death if CMV testing of the fetus or neonate was not performed.

Results

From 2012 to 2018, a total of 206,082 pregnant women were screened for primary CMV infection before 23 weeks of gestation; of the 712 participants (0.35%) who tested positive, 399 (56%) underwent randomization. The trial was stopped early for futility. Data on the primary outcome were available for 394 participants; a primary outcome event occurred in the fetus or neonate of 46 of 203 women (22.7%) in the group that received hyperimmune globulin and of 37 of 191 women (19.4%) in the placebo group (relative risk, 1.17; 95% confidence interval [CI] 0.80 to 1.72; $p = 0.42$). Death occurred in 4.9% of fetuses or neonates in the hyperimmune globulin group and in 2.6% in the placebo group (relative risk, 1.88; 95% CI, 0.66 to 5.41), preterm birth occurred in 12.2% and 8.3%, respectively (relative risk, 1.47; 95% CI, 0.81 to 2.67), and birth weight below the 5th percentile occurred in 10.3% and 5.4% (relative risk, 1.92; 95% CI, 0.92 to 3.99). One participant in the hyperimmune globulin group had a severe allergic reaction to the first infusion. Participants who received hyperimmune globulin had a higher incidence of headaches and shaking chills while receiving infusions than participants who received placebo.

Conclusions

Among pregnant women, administration of CMV hyperimmune globulin starting before 24 weeks' gestation did not result in a lower incidence of a composite of congenital CMV infection or perinatal death than placebo.

(Adapted from "A Trial of Hyperimmune Globulin to Prevent Congenital Cytomegalovirus Infection" by B. L. Hughes et al. in *New England Journal of Medicine*, *385*(5), 2021.)

Abstract 3

We prove for the *N*-body problem the existence of hyperbolic motions for any prescribed limit shape and any given initial configuration of the bodies. The energy level $h > 0$ of the motion can also be chosen arbitrarily. Our approach is based on the construction of global viscosity solutions for the Hamilton-Jacobi equation $H(x, d_x u) = h$. We prove that these solutions are fixed points of the associated Lax-Oleinik semi-group. The presented results can also be viewed as a new application of Marchal's Theorem, whose main use in recent literature has been to prove the existence of periodic orbits.

Keywords: *N*-body problem, Hamilton-Jacobi equation, viscosity solutions

(Adapted from "Viscosity Solutions and Hyperbolic Motions: A New PDE Method for the *N*-body Problem" by E. Maderna & A. Venturelli in *Annals of Mathematics*, *192*(2), 2020.)

Exercises

I. Read the following titles and compare them in terms of format and structure.

(1) Unbiased Identification of Fractional Order System with Unknown Time-delay Using Bias Compensation Method

(2) A Refined Closed-form Solution for Laterally Loaded Circular Membranes in Frictionless Contact with Rigid Flat Plates: Simultaneous Improvement of Out-of-plane Equilibrium Equation and Geometric Equation

(3) Cascade of Care During the First 36 Months of the Treatment as Prevention for Hepatitis C (TraP HepC) Program in Iceland: A Population-based Study

(4) Screening and Remodeling of Enone Oxidoreductase for High Production of 2(or 5)-Ethyl-5(or 2)-methyl-4-hydroxy-3(2H)-Furanone in *Saccharomyces Cerevisiae*

(5) On the Fibration Method for Zero-cycles and Rational Points

II. Translate the following Chinese sentences into English using the appropriate expressions chosen from the box.

- a major area of interest within the field of…
- systematically review…
- reach a mature stage
- aim/attempt/intend to…
- assess/estimate the efficacy of…
- investigate/explore the relationship/association/interaction between…and…
- the primary outcome
- allow for a conclusive interpretation
- the results suggest that…
- we introduce the notion/theory/framework of…

Unit 1 Titles and Abstracts

(1) 本研究旨在评价粒状橡胶和纳米二氧化硅改性沥青的物理和流变性能。
_____
_____

(2) 目前关于地面沉降的理论和应用研究还没有达到成熟阶段。
_____
_____

(3) 这个实验调查了中国东南沿海五省居民的饮食习惯和 2 型糖尿病发病率的关系。
_____
_____

(4) 但是，由于缺乏降雨数据，无法对同位素结果作出结论性的解释。
_____
_____

(5) 实验结果表明，本文提出的 SSFE 方法在合成语音的语音质量和面声匹配度方面均优于目前的方法。
_____
_____

III. Put the following sentences into the right cells of the table according to the discussion on the moves of abstract writing.

A. We directly visualize elongation of the particles, which, by comparison with ensemble X-ray diffraction, allows us to determine changes in the state of charge of individual particles.

B. These results demonstrate the power of optical scattering microscopy to track rapid non-equilibrium processes that would be inaccessible with established characterization techniques.

C. A continuous change in scattering intensity with state of charge enables the observation of non-equilibrium kinetic phase separations within individual particles.

D. To rationalize and improve the performance of newly developed high-rate battery electrode materials, it is crucial to understand the ion intercalation and degradation mechanisms occurring during the realistic battery operation.

E. Phase field modeling (informed by pulsed-field-gradient nuclear magnetic resonance and electrochemical experiments) supports the kinetic origin of this separation, which arises from the state-of-charge dependence of the Li-ion diffusion coefficient.

F. Here we apply a laboratory-based operando optical scattering microscopy method to study micrometer-sized rod-like particles of the anode material $Nb_{14}W_3O_{44}$ during high-rate cycling.

G. The non-equilibrium phase separations lead to particle cracking at high rates of delithiation, particularly in longer particles, with some of the resulting fragments becoming electrically disconnected on subsequent cycling.

(Adapted from "Operando Monitoring of Single-particle Kinetic State-of-charge Heterogeneities and Cracking in High-rate Li-ion Anodes" by A. J. Merryweather et al. in *Nature Material, 8*, 2022.)

Moves	Sentences
Background	
Methods	
Results	
Conclusions	

IV. **Read the following abstract and improve it in terms of language use, style, and structure.**

Objective: To analyze the clinical traits of blood uric acid levels in patients with PD.

Methods: There were a total of 141 patients with PD and 141 health check-up controls from health care department, matched with age, sex, and weight in the present study. All Participants were from Jiangbin Hospital of Guangxi Zhuang Autonomous Region. According to H-Y staging, PD patients were divided into early, middle, and late stages. All participants received the detection of blood uric acid levels.

Results: Lower serum uric acid levels were observed in PD patients compared with controls ($p = 0.009$). There was no significant difference in blood uric acid levels between the PD group and the controls ($p > 0.05$). The blood uric acid levels in patients with late stage PD were higher than early ($p = 0.001$) and middle stages ($p < 0.001$). There was an inverse correlation of serum uric acid levels with H-Y scales in PD patients ($p = 0.001$).

Conclusion: This study has filled the void in the previous research. Blood uric acid may be an important marker of PD and the serum uric acid level could be a biomarker for the progression of PD.

(选自"帕金森病血尿酸水平的临床研",何香花等,《中国老年保健医学》,第12卷,第6期,2018年)

V. Translate the following two Chinese titles and abstracts into English using the expressions listed below.

Excerpt 1

标题:基于合成语音的计算安全隐写方法

摘要:

计算安全的隐写理论很早就被提出,但一直不能用于主流的以多媒体数据为载体的隐写术。原因在于计算安全隐写的前提是可以获得载体的精确分布或可以按照载体分布精确采样,而自然采集的图像、音/视频无法满足这个前提条件。近几年,随着深度学习的发展,多媒体生成技术,例如图像生成和语音合成,逐渐成熟且在互联网上的应用越来越普遍。生成媒体成为合理的隐写载体,隐写者可以用正常的生成媒体掩盖秘密通信,即在媒体生成过程中隐写信息,并与正常的生成媒体不可区分。一些生成模型学到的分布是可知或可控的,这将为计算安全隐写推向实用提供契机。以当前广泛应用的合成语音模型为例,本研究设计并实现了计算安全的对称密钥隐写算法,即在音频生成过程中,根据样本点的条件概率,按算术编码的译码过程将消息解压缩到合成音频中,消息接收方拥有相同的生成模型,通过复现音频合成过程完成消息提取。在该算法的基础上进一步设计了公钥隐写算法,为实现包括隐蔽密钥交换在内的全流程隐蔽通信提供了算法支撑,在保证隐写内容安全的同时,还可以实现隐写行为安全。理论分析显示,文中所提隐写算法的安全性由嵌入消息的随机性决定,隐写分析实验进一步验证了当前技术下攻击者无法区分合成的载体音频与载密音频。

关键词：音频隐写；语音合成；生成模型；公钥隐写

（选自"基于合成语音的计算安全隐写方法"，李梦涵等，《网络与信息安全学报》，第8卷，第3期，2022年）

Some expressions that might be used:

隐写	steganography	多媒体生成	machine-generated
语音合成	speech synthesis	公钥隐写	the public key steganography
载密音频	encrypted audio		

Excerpt 2

标题：基于核磁共振技术的合欢种子吸水特性

摘要：

【目的】采用核磁共振技术，从时间、空间角度探究热水处理后合欢种子的初始吸水位点及水分的动态移动过程，揭示其内部水分相态的变化，为合欢种子吸水特性研究提供一种全新的技术手段。

【方法】对始温80℃热水处理后的合欢种子，用称重法确定种子吸水率，用核磁共振成像技术观察初始吸水位点及水分在种子体内的移动规律，同时结合横向弛豫时间T_2，探究吸水过程中水分相态及其含量、比例的动态变化。

【结果】合欢种子吸水曲线呈S型变化：吸水前期（0～4h）种子吸水率缓慢增加；4～12h进入快速吸水阶段，吸水率增幅较大；吸水12h后进入缓慢吸水期。核磁共振成像结果表明，水分最初从种孔进入种子，然后通过三条路线移动：沿着种皮两侧的维管束向合点端移动；通过种皮与子叶的缝隙向下（合点端）移动，同时进入子叶的外侧；水分通过胚根进入胚轴，由胚轴进入子叶并向合点端移动，但其移动速度明显慢于第二条。整个吸水过程中三种状态水分含量的比例始终处于动态变化中，并且胞外自由水的含量远高于结合水和胞内水。吸水过程中结合水与胞外自由水的峰顶点呈现左移现象（即流动性在减弱）。

【结论】种孔是合欢种子的最初吸水位点，水分进入后通过两侧种皮、种皮与子叶缝隙以及胚轴向合点端移动。吸水过程中，合欢种子中始终存在结合水、胞内水、胞外自由水这三种相态的水，且在整个吸胀过程中相互转化，为种子萌发提供前期准备。

关键词：合欢；吸水；核磁共振技术；水分相态

（改编自"基于核磁共振技术的合欢种子吸水特性"，杜恬恬等，《林业科学》，第 4 期，2022 年）

Some expressions that might be used:

合欢	*Albizia julibrissin (A. julibrissin)*	水分相态	water phase
种皮	seed coat	维管束	vascular bundle
合点	chalazal	子叶	cotyledon
胚根	radicle	胚轴	hypocotyl
胞外自由水	extra-cellular free water	结合水	bound water
胞内水	cytoplasmic bulk water	吸胀	imbibition
种孔	micropyle		

Project

Work in groups. Choose 3–4 articles from different authoritative international journals in your discipline and discuss the wording, style, and organization of the titles and abstracts. Prepare a presentation to be delivered in class.

Unit 2

Introductions

Part I
Introducing the Unit

Introduction is the part of an academic paper which helps the readers understand the writing purpose as well as the background of writing. It is the part which can attract the readers to read further. Clarity, simplicity, and integrity should be important factors to be considered when we write the introduction. An introduction generally begins by citing initial groundbreaking or classical studies related to the area of study, proceeding to other major developments that follow the classical studies, and ending with the gap in the literature, which the research and results will address, as shown by the purpose statement.

The introduction determines the context and significance of the study, and thus provides the readers with general background information at the beginning of the paper. By describing the importance of the relevant research, the authors will help the readers understand the research background, research progress, and contributions of others. Finally, some unsolved questions or the remaining problems should be mentioned as well.

In this unit, by reading, analyzing, and comparing the introductions of some research articles from the academic journals in science and technology, we will learn how to write a proper introduction.

After finishing this unit, you are expected to achieve the following learning objectives:

- to comprehend the basic elements of introductions in academic papers;
- to use signal phrases and typical templates in writing introductions;
- to be acquainted with the procedures, methods, and criterion of writing introductions;
- to understand some methods of writing effective introductions.

Unit 2 Introductions

Part II
Learning Useful Expressions

Study the bold-faced expressions that are often used in the introductions of journal articles.

A. Showing a Research Area

- Modeling is **an important aspect of** XML development.

- In recent years, **rapid advances have been made in** digitalization of information.

- Recently, **there has been increasing interest in** energy storage technology.

- **There is a pressing need to** understand where best to locate future PAs in order to maximize effectiveness and feasibility for biodiversity conservation.

- Meat substitution **is becoming one of the main directions in** the climate improvement strategies for sustainable food systems.

- Concerning meat consumption, **there is a consensus** that consumer preferences are in particular affected by products' sensory characteristics.

- Studies to determine mechanisms underlying the metabolic decompensation in minority populations with a history of hyperglycemic crises are **a major area of interest** within the field of diabetes.

- Higher-order Spectra (HOS) and artificial neural networks **have received considerable attention**.

B. Stating the Value of the Research

- Advanced porous materials are considered to **have broad development prospects in** chemical separations because of their adjustable pore size, high specific surface area, rich reactive sites, and the ability to separate molecules according to the shape and size of the molecules.

- Therefore, **it is crucial to reveal the relationship** between milling force, surface quality, and milling parameters by conducting micro-milling experiments and optimizing the milling parameters to meet the application requirements under the urgent needs of engineering.

- Among the different systems, the realization of quantum circuits on a solid-

27

state quantum chip **is one of the most important and promising routes** towards scalable quantum information processors, and has attracted researchers from a wide range of fields including mathematics, information, chemistry, materials, etc. to join in and carry out interdisciplinary research.

- An area **of particular concern** is water scarcity, which could lead to food shortage and social unrest.

- Moreover, having these edges generally exposed **highlights the importance of** the fold protection panel 108.

- This research **tackles one of the greatest limits of** A systems.

C. Identifying the Research Gap

- However, given the wide confidence intervals for the estimate of effect, the findings do not **allow for a conclusive interpretation**.

- Therefore, pump failure **is one of the major obstacles** for a commercial engine application.

- Therefore, the NGHs distribution **cannot be accurately described** using conventional seismic inversion methods in general.

- Albeit fast and easy to implement, rule-based approaches for detecting human intention tend to have adequate performance **under certain circumstances only** and **cannot easily be generalized to** different pHRI tasks of similar nature.

- Whereas proving to be a highly successful strategy, the eutectic solidification and the in situ conversion process of the composite design **limits** the metal choice of the second phase and **restricts** its volume fraction.

- The above research mainly focuses on the production process of GDP, while **there are only a few studies on** the micro-milling characteristics of GDP materials.

D. Stating the Research Purpose

- Based on this, **this study analyzes** the spatial distribution characteristics and accumulation mode of the NGH-bearing deposits in the area using the inversion results combined with regional geological characteristics.

- The gas load and circulation velocity which may affect the hydrate formation **were also studied to provide basic data for** production design in the following field oceanic hydrate production tests.

- Hence, **this study proposes** a simple, yet effective, and successful range-based estimation of architectural barriers composed of two 360° LIDAR scanners and an effective autonomous climbing state machine based on obstacle classification outputs.
- **The work explores** the influence of process parameters on milling force and surface roughness.
- **Our goal is to successfully develop** various products with specific characteristics for the treatment of many diseases.
- In this study, we **tried to overcome these limitations by** designing an ex situ multilayer Nb/NiTi composite by means of packaged multiple pass roll-bonding.

Part III
Learning Ways of Organization

In this part, we are going to discuss the structures of introductions so as to develop the skills of writing introductions of academic papers in science and technology.

The introduction has three functions as follows: (1) defining the larger general territory or context from which the topic of the study develops; (2) pointing out a gap or lack of knowledge that exists in the literature related to the topic of the study; and (3) indicating how the study fills this gap. To achieve these functions, the introduction should contain the following elements: the status quo of research in the field you are working on, the questions that you raise in the process of research, and the ways you sought to answer the questions and solve the problems. Meanwhile, the main findings in the research can be addressed as well. In order to demonstrate the different functions, the following are three moves recommended in writing an introduction. Within each move, several steps may be adopted.

Move 1 Establishing a Researching Area

Step 1: Describing the General Situation

e.g., In many types of solid tumors, uncontrolled proliferation of tumor cells and dysfunctional vascular growth will lead to hypoxia and acidification of tumors. In addition, dense extracellular matrix as a natural barrier prevents the effective diffusion of nutrients, therapeutic agents, oxygen, and other molecules.

e.g., Taste principally serves two functions: It enables the evaluation of foods for toxicity and nutrients while helping us decide what to ingest and it prepares the body to metabolize foods once they have been ingested.

Step 2: Narrowing down the General Perspective

e.g., As a result, the complex tumor microenvironment (TME) has different physiological characteristics from normal cells/tissues (e.g., acidic pH, reductive conditions, hypoxia, hydrogen peroxide [H_2O_2] overexpression).

e.g., Majority consumes less dietary Ca than recommended value.

Step 3: Focusing on the Specific Area

e.g., By utilizing the above characteristics, nanomaterials with responsiveness towards different TME stimulation have been designed and applied in specific tumor therapy, improving therapeutic efficacy and biological safety.

e.g., Nanoparticles (NPs) are a wide class of materials that include particulate substances, which have one dimension less than 100 nm at least (Laurent et al., 2010).

Step 4: Defining the Specific Terms

e.g., DNA molecules have the dual identities of building materials (self-assembly) and therapeutic agents (gene therapy), realizing the fusion of complex structures and diverse functions.

e.g., Protein glycosylation is an essential and well-studied post-translational modification that requires the sequential addition of single monosaccharides to form a glycan structure.

Move 2 Pointing out Achievements or Problems in the Research Area

Step 1: Summarizing Achievements

e.g., Skeletal reserves of Ca is critical for its structure and is necessary for tissue rigidity, strength, cell permeability as a mineral, secretion of hormones, neuromuscular functioning, activation of enzymes, and development of bones and elasticity.

e.g., DNA nanostructures can be used as matrix to hybrid with protein, organic molecules, liposomes, inorganic nanoparticles, and other materials.

Step 2: Pointing out the Gap

e.g., Owing to the scarcity of articulated dinosaur embryo fossils, it is unclear whether non-avian dinosaurs attained a bird-like posture before hatching, or were more similar to the ancestral archosaurian condition.

e.g., Although evidences showing that stress modulates decision-making is accumulating (Starcke & Brand, 2012; Galvan & Rahdar, 2013, Morgado et al., 2015), there is currently no theoretical framework to explain why stress should influence decisions in certain ways.

Step 3: Identifying a Problem or Need

e.g., Up to now, most defects were identified in the synthesis of Dol-P-Man caused by mutations in DPM3, while recently the CMP-sialic acid transporter SLC35A1 was associated with abnormal O-mannosylation via unknown processes.

e.g., A novel gene defect in the isoprenoid synthase domain containing (ISPD) gene with unknown function was identified in patients with deficient α-DG O-mannosylation (Roscioli et al., 2012; Willer et al., 2012), displaying a heterogeneous spectrum of phenotypes.

Move 3 Evaluating the Current Research

Step 1: Describing the Purpose of Research

e.g., Our objective was to assess the effect of a "credit card" adult asthma self-management plan in a community experiencing major health problems from asthma, by means of a before-and-after intervention trial of the efficacy of the "credit card" plan, when introduced through community-based asthma clinics.

e.g., The aim of this paper is to investigate and assess the implications of current practice among large U.K. companies in relation to the award of annual bonuses to senior executives.

Step 2: Explaining the Methods

e.g., Microtomographic measurement was used to consider the complicated shape of the external surfaces of the struts and the internal microporosity. Based on the tomographic images, the realistic shape of the examined structures was recreated.

e.g., Thus, to investigate this interaction, we first examined the effect of a series of temperatures on the mixtures of certain ratios of C/N (25), and secondly, compared the digestion performance of mixtures with a series of C/N ratios by adjusting the proportions of each substrate, dairy manure (DM), chicken manure (CM), and rice straw (RS) under mesophilic and thermophilic conditions.

Step 3: Demonstrating the Value of Research Findings

e.g., Experiments suggested an influence of ISPD mutations on protein O-mannosyltransferase (POMT) activity, and an additive effect with dystroglycanopathy genes.

e.g., Compared with other nanomaterials, DNA nanomaterials have superior characteristics.

The following introduction is taken from an article published in the *Applied Food Research*. It shows how the three-move structure is applied.

① Snacks are quick foods usually derived from one or more basic food items, and are eaten between meals. ② Snack foods have become a significant part of the diet of many individuals, particularly children, and can influence overall nutrition. ③ There is a growing consumer interest in ready-to-eat snack foods mainly due to their convenience, wide availability, appearance, taste, and texture. ④ Population-based studies have shown increased food consumption related to the snacking habits (Shukla, 1994). ⑤ In recent years, the food market has been fast adapting to diversified needs and requirements of a contemporary consumer. ⑥ The proceeding economic, social, and cultural changes have resulted in an increased demand of consumers for the so-called "convenient food". ⑦ The concept of convenient food encompasses food products obtained upon such processing of raw material that enables using it for fast, convenient, and easy preparation of meals. ⑧ The group of convenient foodstuffs includes, among others, prepared cereal-flour products, e.g., extruded snacks (Rytel et al., 2013). ⑨ Cereal snacks are traditionally considered unhealthy because they contain high sugar or high fat levels and low essential nutrients. ⑩ This has led the food industry to develop novel and healthier products like fortified snacks with functional ingredients for health conscious consumers (Popkin & Duffey, 2010). ⑪ Extrusion is a high temperature short-time process which involves simultaneous thermal and pressure treatment along with mechanical shearing, resulting in changes such as gelatinization of starch, denaturation of protein, and at times complete cooking of the extrudates to obtain ready-to-eat products (Singh et al., 2007).

⑫ Many extruded products are mostly made from cereals such as corn, rice, and wheat. ⑬ These cereals are rich in carbohydrates and fibers but relatively low in protein content; thus they need to enhance the protein component in the extruded products (Mahungu et al.,1999). ⑭ Due to consumer demand for healthy extruded snack foods, many industries have increased focus in research and product development to produce products that are nutrient-dense (Brennan, 2011). ⑮ Cereals and legumes, in general, play an important role in human nutrition. ⑯ Recent studies have shown that cereals and beans contain constituents that have health benefits for humans, such as antioxidants and anti-disease factors (Ragaee et al., 2006). ⑰ Corn is the main cereal grain as measured by production but ranks third as a staple food, after wheat and rice. ⑱ Corn grits are the main raw material for commercial production of extruded snacks. ⑲ They have high porosity, crunchy texture, and are palatable (Ascheri & Elaboraçao, 2003). ⑳ Many formulated products are based on wheat flour (among other components) and its popularity is largely determined by the ability of the wheat flour to be processed into different products, for example, a snack, which is mainly given by the unique properties of wheat-flour gluten proteins (Anjum et al., 2007). ㉑ Extruded snack products are predominantly made from cereal flour or starches and tend to be low in protein and have a low biological value (i.e., low concentration of essential amino acids)

(Ainsworth et al., 2007).

㉒ Rice flour prepared from rice broken has become an ingredient of interest for many ready-to-eat breakfast cereals and snacks due to its bland taste, attractive white color, hypoallergenicity, and easy of digestion (Chaiyakul et al., 2009). ㉓ Guha & Ali (2006) reported that the glutinous rice was a suitable material to produce the expanded extrudate rice product such as ready-to-eat snacks, and breakfast cereals, with low bulk density, high expansion, and low shear stress. ㉔ Chickpea (Cicer arietinum L.) is globally the third most important pulse crop after navy beans and dry beans. ㉕ The subspecies arietinum is divided into two distinct types (i.e., Kabuli or Garbanzo type and Desi type). ㉖ Kabuli chickpeas are of Mediterranean and Middle Eastern origin (Petterson et al., 1997). ㉗ Chickpeas contain moderately high protein (17%–22%), low fat (6.48%), high available carbohydrate (50%), and crude fiber contents of 3.82% on dry basis. ㉘ Hence, chickpea seeds can play an important role as a low-glycemic functional ingredient in a healthy diet (Saleh & El-Adawy, 2006). ㉙ The parched chickpea has an attractive golden—yellow color, a porous texture, and a pleasant taste (Ziena, 2007). ㉚ Wide cultivation and spread of faba bean (Vicia faba L.) in the temperate and subtropical regions has ranked it the fourth most important legume crop in the world, next to dry beans, dry peas, and chickpeas (Alghamdi, 2009). ㉛ Vicia faba is a sustainable protein source with a great potential in nutritional and functional properties (Multari et al., 2015).

㉜ This study was carried out to prepare and evaluate six different snack samples characterized by high nutritional value based on local available ingredients cereals (yellow corn, wheat flour, and broken rice), legumes (decorticated parched chickpea and faba bean cotyledons), and skimmed milk powder by extrusion technique. ㉝ The chemical composition, minerals, physical properties, amino acids, C-PER, peroxide value, and sensory evaluation of snacks were determined.

(Adapted from "Nutritious Novel Snacks from Some of Cereals, Legumes, and Skimmed Milk Powder" by H. M. Ziena & A. H. M. Ziena in *Applied Food Research*, 2(1), 2022.)

The first part in the introduction (Sentences ①–⑤) functions as Move 1 (Establishing a Researching Area). In this move, the authors start the topic by defining snack foods or "convenient" foods in Sentences ①–③ (Move 1, Step 1), and then narrow it down to convenient and healthy snack foods in Sentences ④–⑤ (Move 1, Step 2). The authors start by giving a definition to the larger or general context in which the study develops and then point out the gap between the past research and the current research. Thus, an explanation of the research can help readers understand the writing purpose. On the basis of the background information, the authors also explain the necessity of the research on this topic, that is, "Why should people pay attention to this topic?" These illustrations can be seen in Sentences ⑥–⑦ (Move 1, Step 3). And even in the Introduction part, the advantages and disadvantages of six snack foods are mentioned in an orderly way. They are brief but clearly-cut descriptions. The purpose of the research is listed as Sentences ⑧–⑲ (Move 2, Step 1) and the readers may have a clear map of the functions of six snack foods. In addition, the properties of six snack foods are illustrated and compared with detailed figures in Sentences ⑳–㉛ (Move 2, Step 2). Finally, the last part, which includes Sentences ㉜–㉝ (Move 3, Step 3), illustrates that the focus of the research will be on the "chemical composition, minerals, physical properties, amino acids, C-PER, peroxide value, and sensory evaluation of snacks".

There are some tips on how to write the introduction:

- To write an effective introduction, we need to adopt a certain strategy for beginning it. Since the introduction of a science paper always starts with the most general items, it tends to be the most general and abstract section of the paper. However, there are still certain repeated patterns. First, briefly introduce the research background and then move on to the theme. Another common way for beginning the introduction is to provide a definition of an important scientific term. In addition, the introduction may focus on indicating a problem with positive or negative social effects.

- We need to narrow the focus and clarify the specific scope of research that describes the gap, drawbacks, and problems. In addition to certain common nouns used to discuss a problem, some verbs are also commonly used. First, summarize the research status of the subject and then explain the contribution the research has made to the academic field. When summarizing the research status quo, we can quote some of the most relevant literature, and point out how the research will fill the theoretical gap in this field, or how the research will solve practical problems.

- We also need to make a generalization and see what kind of conclusion the readers can get from the research. A summary of what others have done in the field will help the editor provide further revision. Thus, it should be added in the Introduction part.

Part IV
Analyzing the Examples

In this part, we are going to analyze some examples so as to understand the wording, structures, and moves of introductions of academic papers in science and technology.

I. Analyze the following introduction and discuss the questions with a partner.

In the last decades, numerous new energy storage systems drew great attention, due to rising energy demands of global population. Electrical double layer capacitors (EDLCs) and lithium-ion batteries (LIBs) are the promising electrochemical systems for future applications in electromobility, portable electronic systems, and storing of excess energy in power grids. They are able to store charges quickly and efficiently, thus helping to generate renewable energy and convert it into a usable form. EDLCs especially are electrochemical systems to provide energy in a fast and reliable manner due to high capacitance and cycling numbers as well as fast charging and discharging mechanisms based on electrostatic interactions, specific adsorption, and reversible electron transfers. To remain these characteristics, the faultless operation of the system has to ensure and depends significantly on the electrode material. Because of its chemical stability, high adsorption properties, and high specific area, activated carbon (AC) became a suitable material considering EDLC electrodes. Recently, efforts have been made to obtain low-cost carbon-based materials for the convenient and practical application in electrochemical devices. In this case, biomass became an attractive precursor for carbon electrodes besides conventional materials such as ceramic, polymers, and metal oxides. An interesting field of research is the suitability of agricultural residues as an abundant and renewable resource for EDLC electrode materials. The application of technical processes enables the conversion of the starting materials into highly porous carbon products. In those terms, thermochemical syntheses as hydrothermal carbonization (HTC) and pyrolysis/chemical activation are beneficial for functionalization of organic matter like biomass and agricultural residues. HTC takes place in a closed system within a temperature range between 170 °C and 350 °C. Throughout this process, the initial carbon matrix of the bio-based starting materials underlies numerous parallel and consecutive reactions such as dehydration, decarboxylation, polymerization, and aromatization. Yet, the kinetics of these cascades of reactions are not fully understood. However, the hydrothermal decomposition of biopolymers of the biomass leads to restructuring of the carbon matrix on a molecular basis and building of an aromatic carbon network with abundant functional groups, called hydrochar (HC). Also, the modification of these char-like products with nanoparticles can have an influence in the carbon material properties. Carbon materials can promote the formation of core-shell nanostructures by encapsulating metal oxides (e.g., SnO_2, Fe_2O_3, Fe_3O_4) present during hydrothermal carbonization. A following pyrolysis or activation treatment at high temperatures between 500 °C and 900 °C provides better adherence to the carbon matrix. Moreover, activation leads into formation of highly porous carbon with high surface areas and enhanced adsorption properties that are crucial for the characteristics of EDLC-electrodes.

In the last decade, several studies reported on the preparation of functionalized carbon materials and EDLC electrodes derived from banana fibers, cashmere, coconut shells, coffee grounds, starch, and corncob while applying these methods. However, carbonaceous materials are still facing drawbacks regarding their utilization as electrodes for supercapacitors. For instance, ACs can suffer from poor permittivity and polarization ability as well as low electrical conductivity due to its amorph character. Redox-active species like Fe_2O_3, Fe_3O_4, MnO_2, NiO, and RuO_2 influence the energy storage mechanisms occurring at the electrode surface. These so-called pseudocapacitors enable charge transfers (faradaic currents) due to reversible redox reactions between the electrode and the electrolyte species. In contrast, EDLCs only provide double layer capacitance due to electron transfers of the adsorbed charge carriers. Thus, it has been reported that heteroatom doping and insertion of MO nanoparticles can improve the electrochemical performance of the device due to the reversible charge storage.

In this study, we examine the physicochemical properties and electrochemical performance of bio-based electrode materials, as well as the carbon and mass balance, which serve as a basis for life cycle assessment. A good sustainability of the process could only be reached if no or not much carbon is lost during conversion. Therefore, the two organic residual biomasses, bakery waste (BW) and spent coffee grounds (SCG) have been chosen as precursors. HTC pretreatment with in situ doping of Fe_2O_3-, Fe_3O_4-, and MnO_2-nanoparticles and a subsequent activation process were carried out to obtain activated carbon containing metal oxides. The influence of the selected biomasses and metal oxide nanoparticles on thermochemical processes and electrochemistry were evaluated. The production of "green" electrode materials represents a future-orientated and sustainable route within a bioeconomy concept.

(Adapted from "Metal Oxide-doped Activated Carbons from Bakery Waste and Coffee Grounds for Application in Supercapacitors" by P. Konnerth et al. in *Materials Science for Energy Technologies, 4,* 2021.)

 Questions:

1. Which sentence is the topic sentence of the introduction?

2. What tenses and voices are used in the introduction? Why are they used?

3. What is the function of the last sentence?

II. Compare the following two introductions and answer the questions.

Introduction 1

① Virus infections initiate with binding of viral particles to host surface cellular receptors. ② Receptor recognition is therefore an important determinant of the cell and tissue tropism of a virus. ③ In addition, the gain of function of a virus to bind to the receptor counterparts in other species is also a prerequisite for inter-species transmission (Lu et al., 2015). ④ Interestingly, with the exception of HCoV-OC43 and HKU1, both of which have been shown to engage sugars for cell attachment (Li et al., 2005), the other human CoVs recognize proteinaceous peptidases as receptors. ⑤ HCoV-229E binds to human aminopeptidase N (hAPN) (Li et al., 2019), and

MERS-CoV interacts with human dipeptidyl peptidase (hDPP4 or hCD26) (Lu et al., 2013; Raj et al., 2013). ⑥ Although they belong to different genera, SARS-CoV and hCoV-NL63 interact with human angiotensin-converting enzyme 2 (hACE2) for virus entry (Hofmann et al., 2005; Li et al., 2003; Wu et al., 2009). ⑦ After the outbreak of COVID-19, Chinese scientists promptly determined that SARS-CoV-2 also utilizes hACE2 for cell entry (Zhou et al., 2020).

⑧ In CoVs, the entry process is mediated by the envelope-embedded surface-located spike (S) glycoprotein (Lu et al., 2015). ⑨ This S protein would, in most cases, be cleaved by host proteases into the S1 and S2 subunits, which are responsible for receptor recognition and membrane fusion, respectively (Lai et al., 2007). ⑩ S1 can be further divided into an N-terminal domain (NTD) and a C-terminal domain (CTD), both of which can function as a receptor-binding entity (e.g., SARS-CoV and MERS-CoV utilize the S1 CTD to recognize the receptor [also called receptor binding domain (RBD)] (Li et al., 2005; Lu et al., 2013), whereas mouse hepatitis CoV engages the receptor with its S1 NTD [Taguchi & Hirai-Yuki, 2012]). ⑪ The region in SARS-CoV-2 S protein that is responsible for hACE2 interaction remains unknown.

(Adapted from "Performance Characteristics of Five Immunoassays for SARS-CoV-2: A Head-to-head Benchmark Comparison" by The National SARS-CoV-2 Serology Assay Evaluation Group, in *The Lancet, Infectious Diseases*, 20(12), 2020.)

Introduction 2

冠状病毒近二十年来共造成三次大暴发，此次出现的新冠病毒（SARS-CoV-2）较 2003 年的严重急性呼吸综合征冠状病毒（SARS-CoV）和 2012 年的中东呼吸综合征冠状病毒（MERS-CoV）而言，具有高度传染性、较高隐蔽性和广泛组织趋向性等特征。冠状病毒是一个高度多样化的单股正链 RNA 病毒家族，SARS-CoV-2 属于 β 冠状病毒。在基因组水平上，SARS-CoV-2 与 SARS-CoV 的序列有 79.6% 相同，与蝙蝠冠状病毒的序列有 96% 相同。人类血管紧张素转化酶 2（angiotensin-converting enzyme 2, ACE2）是由 X 染色体基因编码的锌-金属肽酶，属于 I 型跨膜糖蛋白，含有 N 端信号肽、C 端结构域和有催化活性的胞外结构域。ACE2 是 SARS-CoV-2 的受体，SARS-CoV-2 S 蛋白的受体结合结构域（receptor binding domain, RBD）可与人体细胞表明的 ACE2 相互作用而引起感染。因此，ACE2 对于 SARS-CoV-2 的预防、诊断和治疗具有重要意义。研究发现，SARS-CoV 和 MERS-CoV 分别通过果子狸和单峰骆驼直接传播给人类，而且这两种病毒被认为起源于蝙蝠、水貂突变株的发现表明，SARS-CoV-2可以在其他的动物宿主中复制并传播，因此新冠病毒具有通过其他动物扩大传播的潜在风险。然而截至目前，SARS-CoV-2的宿主范围以及中间宿主仍不明确，我们对受体ACE2作用机制的认识仍然有限。为此，本文对不同物种的ACE2蛋白进行同源性及进化性分析，以期为确定新冠病毒的宿主范围提供参考。对ACE2蛋白结构与功能的系统生信分析和原核表达，有助于阐明其作为受体介导病毒入侵的分子机制，为SARS-CoV-2感染的治疗提供一定的理论支持。

（选自"新冠病毒受体蛋白ACE2结构与功能的生信分析及原核表达"，刘玲等，《中国免疫杂志学》，2021年）

 Questions:

1. What are the similarities between the English and the Chinese introductions?

2. What are the differences between them?

3. Can you underline the expressions in Introduction 1 that narrow down the general topic?

4. Which are the signal words that indicate the sequence of research in Introduction 1?

III. Analyze the following introduction and discuss the questions with a partner.

① The intestinal tract is an important digestive and immune organ in the human body. ② Unhealthy intestinal tract affects metabolism, immunity, and mental condition, and the microorganisms that occupy in the intestinal tract was the reason. ③ Intestinal bacteria constitute the gut microbial community, that provides energy and nutrition; protects the integrity of the intestinal structure; and maintains intestinal immunity, including resistance to pathogenic bacteria. ④ Generally, the host, intestinal flora, and external environment maintain a dynamic balance. ⑤ Dysbiosis causes many common and severe diseases. ⑥ Probiotics, employed as immune activators targeting prokaryotic and eukaryotic cells, stimulate and improve the immune system mainly by improving the activity of intestinal flora and the production of effector molecules. ⑦ So far, the mechanism of action of probiotics on the intestinal microecosystems has been classified into five patterns—modulation of endogenous colonies, protection of the intestinal tract barrier, maintenance of homeostasis, regulation of the immune system, and influence on vagal afferents. ⑧ Earlier studies focused mainly on the direct effects of probiotics on the gut microbiota. ⑨ Treatment with Bacillus subtilis CU1 and B. subtilis DSM32315 enhanced the immune system in elderly people and the gut barrier in pigs, respectively. ⑩ Lactobacillus casei Shirota activated vagal afferents to regulate the brain and reduce stress. ⑪ Supplementation of probiotics is beneficial to the recovery and reconstruction of the intestinal flora via several effector molecules, which in turn alleviates diseases and enhances the immune system. ⑫ Lactobacillus brevis B50 reportedly increases the expression of genes related to effector molecules. ⑬ However, there is little evidence to systematically support the specific mechanisms of probiotics in the gut microenvironment. ⑭ In this review, multiple probiotics were investigated to determine how they modulate the secretion of effector molecules and interact with the gut bacteria and improve the homeostasis of the intestine, as well as advance the prospects for probiotics.

(Adapted from "Modulation of Gut Health Using Probiotics: The Role of Probiotic Effector Molecules" by X. Gao et al. in *Journal of Future Foods*, *2*(1), 2022.)

 Questions:

1. Can you underline the topic sentence of the introduction?
2. Can you point out the sentences that make contrast and comparison?
3. Which sentence demonstrates the gap in the current research?

Exercises

I. **Choose the appropriate words in the parentheses to complete the sentences.**

(1) A (perplexing, looming) feature of insomnia is that people seem to overestimate their sleep loss.

(2) The fear of a(n) (outstanding, long-standing) danger became the subject of a large scale photo project.

(3) Protecting the Earth is a (lighthearted, daunting) challenge facing all nations.

(4) Preparing a CV is the first (hurdle, culprit) in a job search.

(5) The (ever-lasting, sustainable) "functional" arrangement of people and machines on the factory floor was to be dismantled.

(6) Smallpox, a (wreck, scourge) of previous generations, now is effectively extinct.

(7) Repeated population (pitfalls, bottlenecks) lead to losses in genetic variation because of random genetic drift.

(8) The knee injury caused a serious (setback, oversight) to his football career.

(9) False appearance and (obstacles, drawbacks) in seismic data often cause wrong interpretations in reservoir description.

(10) This paper analyzes and extends the (unstable, suspending) air model.

II. **Fill in the blanks with the words according to the context of the following introduction. The first letter of each word has been given.**

On January 30, 2020, the World Health Organization d____(1)____ a novel coronavirus, COVID-19, a matter of Public Health Emergency of International Concern. S____(2)____ the rapid growth of infections and deaths, governments

Unit 2 Introductions

worldwide were quick to implement a variety of measures. Among them, technological solutions in the form of anonymized phone location tracking and contact tracing apps.

The use of technology has a___(3)___ a pre-existing debate in Europe regarding the privacy protection of users. In recent years, the European Union has established numerous limitations to the exploitation of personal data. This includes, for example, the limitation on an indiscriminate sharing of personal data with U.S. companies. In 2014, a major court case e___(4)___ a "right to be forgotten" protecting users from indefinite retention of their data on online search platforms. This was followed in 2015 by the Schrems case, in which the Safe Harbor decision was revoked and the transfer of personal data of EU citizens to servers in the U.S. was largely limited. Most recently, the General Data Protection Regulation (GDPR) of 2016 s___(5)___ a groundbreaking and high standard of data protection. Therefore, the use of phone location data to track people's movements and the emergence of contact tracing apps have both sparked concerns.

This paper d___(6)___ the use of technology as a response to the COVID-19 pandemic among the European Union Member States considering years-long European effort to increase privacy protection. This paper i___(7)___ two waves of technological solutions: first, the use of anonymized location data shared by telecommunications companies (hereinafter: telecoms) to m___(8)___ crowd movements; second, the emergence of contact tracing apps to speed up the procedure of identifying infected individuals. Both waves of technological solutions are discussed in terms of p___(9)___, t___(10)___, and effectiveness.

(Adapted from "The COVID-19 Pandemic: Two Waves of Technological Responses in the European Union" by K. Klonowska & P. Bindt in Hague Center for Strategic Studies, 2020.)

III. Translate the following Chinese sentences into English using the appropriate expressions chosen from the box.

- combine medical tools with medical device
- it is generally believed to/that…
- undertake such a complex initiative…

43

- one of the main directions...
- be based on...
- with convenient supply of materials
- less interference with
- it is a long way from...

(1) 我们将运用生物再生医学方法，并结合其他通常用于刺激中枢神经系统的医疗手段，治疗患有其他严重意识障碍的病人。

_____

_____

(2) 坝体所用材料可分为土坝和堆石坝。前者以当地土料、沙、沙砾、卵石为主；后者以石渣、卵石、爆破石料为主。

_____

_____

(3) 复活大脑的几个部分也许还有可能，但若要复活整个大脑，使其功能运转正常且完好无损，则还有很长的路要走。

_____

_____

(4) 人们普遍认为食品生产——特别是肉类和奶制品——是全球环境变化的主要因素。

_____

_____

(5) 高效、高稳定性的弹性阻抗反演已成为地震叠前反演的主要方向之一。

_____

_____

IV. The following sentences come from the introduction of an academic paper and are in scrambled order. Rearrange them to make a coherent paragraph.

A. In recent decades, rapid changes in the health status of children and adults have occurred in most developed countries.

Unit 2 Introductions

B. They do not provide information, however, about why, when, under what circumstances, human consumers select certain foods, why they eat enough or too much of them, why they succeed or fail in adapting their behavior to the conditions of the present-day environment.

C. This is why we should study human food intake behavior.

D. This kind of information is provided by behavior science.

E. Food intake behavior is broadly defined as any food-related response to stimulation from the "internal milieu" or from the environment (Basdevant, Le Barzic, & Guy-Grand, 1990).

F. An increase in the prevalence of several chronic diseases, such as obesity and even Type 2 diabetes, affects all age groups.

G. Such responses can be very simple reflexes, for example, the simple conditioned reflexes described by Pavlov (1927) a century ago, or they can be very complex organized, deliberate responses that will make it possible for an organism to cover its nutritional and energy needs.

H. In addition, behavior itself, beyond whatever the subject thinks and declares about it, must be quantified using validated instruments.

I. Studying scientific disciplines such as nutrition and physiology can reveal what happens in the digestive tract to account for the breakdown of adaptive processes that should protect homeostasis and health.

J. In human eaters, food intake behavior includes the activities of selecting and purchasing a wide variety of foods, organizing meal patterns and actual ingestion.

K. Such declarations, for example, the subject's answers to a questionnaire, must be treated in a way that allows rigorous quantification.

L. The scientific approach requires a precise quantitative assessment of any form of behavior under investigation.

M. It therefore implies social interactions, cognitive tasks (for evaluation of costs or counting calories, for example), psychological attitudes (such as long-term preferences and beliefs), habits and responses to sensory stimulation, among many other influences.

N. These diseases are strongly associated with energy intake and food choices.

O. Precise methods must be used in order to obtain quantitative data describing both the behavior itself and the environment in which it is observed.

P. Precise quantification of these parameters can allow a rational investigation of human eating behavior, its determinants, and its nutritional effects.

Q. The environment is described in terms of setting (natural, social, free-living, laboratory, etc.), time (day, week, year, etc.), and all other potentially relevant dimensions.

R. Ingestive behavior is assessed in terms of type (eating, drinking, avoiding, rejecting, etc.), frequency, size, structure, intensity, and in terms of its numerous contingency relationships with environmental factors.

(Adapted from "How and Why Should We Study Ingestive Behaviors in Humans?" by F. Bellisle in *Food Quality and Preference*, *20*(8), 2009.)

Order: _____

V. **Read the following introduction and find out its problems. Exchange your views with your partner and discuss how to improve it.**

In the field of plant biology, one of the fundamental processes of life is photosynthesis. This process occurs through the fixation of carbon dioxide in the presence of water and may or may not require light (photosynthetic dark reactions can occur in the absence of light). The end result of photosynthesis is the production of organic materials, such as sugars and oxygen, which are necessary for the life processes of many organisms. Although the majority of plants carry out photosynthesis, they do so at different rates. The rate of photosynthesis is dependent upon several environmental factors, including temperature, amount of light present, amount of carbon dioxide present, and the color of the light. In this lab, the purpose was to manipulate one environmental factor to determine the effect on the process of photosynthesis. It was decided that the environmental factor to be tested would be the concentration of carbon dioxide initially present. Then a hypothesis was generated: An increase in the concentration of carbon dioxide initially present will lead to an increase in the rate of photosynthesis, and as a result, an increase in the amount of oxygen generated.

Throughout the experiments, the aquatic plant Elodea was used to carry out photosynthesis. This particular plant is especially conducive to scientific experiments involving photosynthesis because of its ability to produce oxygen bubbles as it carries out photosynthesis, making it simple to monitor the rate of photosynthesis in an experiment.

(Retrieved from the Michigan Corpus of Upper-level Student Papers website.)

Project

Work in groups. Excerpt 1 demonstrates the aftershock sequence of an earthquake. Excerpt 2 lists different opinions on the relation between biodiversity and food security. Except 3 illustrates the properties of topological insulator. Read these excerpts carefully and discuss their wording, style, and organization respectively. Prepare a presentation to be delivered in class.

Excerpt 1

On January 8, 2022, at 1:45 a.m. (Beijing time), a $M_s6.9$ earthquake struck near Menyuan County, Haibei Prefecture, Qinghai Province (hereinafter referred to as the "Menyuan earthquake"). The China Earthquake Networks Center reported the earthquake's focal depth to be at 10 km (37.77°N, 101.26°E). The Qinghai Seismic Network recorded 1,434 aftershocks until 0:00 on January 11, including one earthquake of a magnitude > $M_s5.0$, two of ≥ $M_s4.0$, and 13 of $M_s3.0$. The largest aftershock ($M_s5.1$) was recorded on January 8 at 2:09 a.m., which caused a 22-km surface rupture. The highest intensity was estimated at IX degrees, and the area with an intensity of VI or above was measured to be approximately 23,417 km^2.

The Menyuan earthquake occurred at the intersection of the Lenglongling (LLL) fault and the Tuolaishan (TLS) fault. Strike-slip, thrust, primary, and secondary faults form a complex tectonic system close to the earthquake's epicenter. It is an important part of an almost 1,000-km-long left-lateral strike-slip fault zone at the northeastern margin of the Tibetan Plateau (NETP), which controls the northeastward compression movement of the plateau relative to the Alashan block. The Menyuan earthquake was the largest destructive earthquake to occur near the LLL fault since the 2016 Menyuan M_S6.4 earthquake. At the LLL fault, seismicity is strong and at least six strong earthquakes have occurred along this fault, the largest being the 1927 M_S8.0 Gulang earthquake. Shortly after the Menyuan earthquake, the focal mechanism, rupture process, and high-precision aftershock relocation were studied by domestic and foreign research institutions; however, the seismogenic fault geometry and spatial and temporal evolution of the aftershock sequence remain unclear. In this study, we investigated the precise locations of the aftershock sequence based on seismic data from the Qinghai Seismic Network. Our results provide a reference for determining the seismogenic fault of the Menyuan earthquake, analyzing the characteristics of the earthquake sequence, and determining the earthquake trend.

(Adapted from "High-precision Relocation of the Aftershock Sequence of the January 8, 2022, M_S6.9 Menyuan Earthquake" by L. Fan et al in *Earthquake Science, 35*(2), 2022.)

Excerpt 2

The United Nations Sustainable Development Goal 2 aims to end hunger and achieve food security (Godfray et al., 2010). Faced with rapidly growing crop demand, expansion and intensification of agricultural land has become a prevailing phenomenon (Foley et al., 2005), since technical limitations (Tester & Langridge, 2010) and negative synergies from increasing yield (Phalan et al., 2016) hinder the strategy which aims to increase yield and then spare land for wild nature. Besides agriculture, urban expansion changes land use and exerts cumulatively negative impacts on nature (Mcdonald et al., 2008). As a result, increasing land use intensity and more resources (such as water, pesticides, and fertilizer) inputs for agriculture will lead to the loss, fragmentation, and degradation of natural habitats (Tilman et al., 2001), contributing to global biodiversity decline (Butchart et al., 2010). Specifically, species richness will be seriously threatened due to the expansion of human footprint (Newbold et al., 2015). In this context, satisfying food demands while conserving biodiversity simultaneously is crucial to the global sustainable development (Tscharntke et al., 2012). The conservation of species richness depends on effective conservation and restoration measures (Newbold et al., 2015), especially strategies targeted at species and habitats vulnerable to future environmental changes (Pereira et al., 2010). Hence, conflict risk hotspots between biodiversity conservation and food security need to be identified (Molotoks et al., 2017). Studies which integrated and analyzed species richness of different taxonomic classes as a whole may miss conflict risk hotspots essential for one specific taxonomic class (Kehoe et al., 2017; Shackelford et al., 2015; Sonter et al., 2020). Of the few studies which took different taxonomic classes into account, most mainly focused on the relationship between land use changes related to agriculture and biodiversity, ignoring dramatic urban growth and its potential impacts on nature (Delzeit et al., 2017; Zabel et al., 2019). In this study, we aim to uncover future spatial relationships between land use intensity and species richness of mammals, birds, and amphibians, and to identify global future conflict risk hotspots between biodiversity conservation and food security. To do this, we calculate the Land Use Intensity Index (LUII), which takes both agricultural land and urban area into consideration (Jiang & Yu, 2019; Peng et al., 2016). Land use's potential impacts on species richness of birds, mammals, and amphibians (Jenkins et al., 2013; Pimm et al., 2014) are assessed separately. Then we identify High-High spatial clusters between biodiversity and LUII using local indicators of spatial association (LISA) (Anselin, 1995) at 10-km resolution. These High-High spatial clusters imply locations where high species richness are threatened by land use intensification. We subsequently identify future high spatial auto-correlation (HSA) areas for countries and BHs. Countries and BHs with high proportion of HSA areas and low value of Global Food Security Index (GFSI) are defined as conflict risk hotspots, demanding forward-looking measures and effective management.

(Adapted from "Future Global Conflict Risk Hotspots Between Biodiversity Conservation and Food Security: 10 Countries and 7 Biodiversity Hotspots" by J. Zhao et al. in *Global Ecology and Conservation, 34*, 2022.)

Excerpt 3

Since the discovery of topological insulator (TI), it has drawn a lot of research concentrations due to its novel properties. Three dimensional (3D) TI behaves as an insulator in the bulk but keeps to be metallic at the surface, which is characterized as topological surface states (TSSs) between energy gap. The TSS electrons are massless Dirac fermions with linear energy-momentum dispersion that are protected by time-reversal symmetry. Due to strong spin-orbit coupling (SOC), the TSS electron spins are locked perpendicular to the crystal momentum. Ideally, the TSS electrons are predicted to be immune from backscattering between their time-reversal partner states with opposite momentum because of their opposite spin configurations. Therefore, 3D TI has been proposed to have important applications in spintronics.

Recently, optical excitation technique has been exploited to 3D TI revealing new physics through the coupling of TSS electrons, photons, and phonons. Time and angle-resolved photoemission spectroscopy enables us to observe the ultrafast non-equilibrium carrier dynamics in 3D TI. After optical excitation, SOC and electron-phonon (e-ph) coupling come into play collectively in the relaxation dynamic process, generating different relaxation channels. For example, electrons that are excited to conduction bands (CBs) are found to relax to TSS within picoseconds (ps). The timescale depends on the temperature, implying a major role of e-ph coupling. Electrons that are excited to higher energy TSS will relax to the Fermi level in an ultrafast manner. More interestingly, it was reported that the spin relaxes much faster than the charge. Both the e-ph and the electron-electron scattering mechanisms were proposed. A recent study shows that the asymmetric electron population on TSS generated by circularly polarized optical excitation decays within 165 fs, suggesting an ultrafast scattering between the time-reversal pair TSSs. To achieve a comprehensive understanding on the non-equilibrium carrier and spin dynamics in 3D TI, a state-of-art ab initio investigation is essential.

The development of time-domain ab initio non-adiabatic molecular dynamics (NAMD) makes such study possible, and we choose a prototypical 3D TI Bi_2Se_3 to investigate. We prove the strong temperature dependence of the carrier relaxation from TSSs to bulk CBs, suggesting a dominating role of e-ph coupling. More strikingly, we reveal that backscattering can happen between time-reversal pair TSSs during the non-equilibrium dynamics. It is driven by spin canting induced by e-ph coupling and SOC collectively. Both the spin canting and the backscattering result in the ultrafast spin relaxation with a timescale around 100 fs. Our simulation provides critical insights into the non-equilibrium electron and spin dynamics in 3D TI.

(Adapted from "Excited Electron and Spin Dynamics in Topological Insulator: A Perspective from Ab Initio Non-adiabatic Molecular Dynamics" by C. Zhao et al in *Fundamental Research*, 2(4), 2022.)

Unit 3

Methodological Descriptions

Part I
Introducing the Unit

In a typical IMRaD structure (introduction-methods-results-discussion) of the research paper, the Methods section is the most important part as it provides a clear description of how the research was done, what was done to answer the research question, and how the results were analyzed. To be more specific, the Methods section is intended to describe the actions taken to investigate a research problem and explain the rationale for the application of specific procedures or techniques used to identify, select, process, and analyze the information applied to understand the problem. It must be written with enough information so that the research could be repeated by others to evaluate whether or not the results are reproducible, and the readers can judge whether or not the results and conclusions are valid.

In this unit, we will learn how to write methodological descriptions of research articles in science and technology, including the content, organization, and language style of the Methods section.

After finishing this unit, you are expected to achieve the following learning objectives:

- to understand the organizational patterns and the rhetorical moves in the Methods section in a research article;
- to use signal phrases and typical expressions in writing methodological descriptions;
- to learn how to write methodological descriptions in research articles in your discipline.

Unit 3 Methodological Descriptions

Part II
Learning Useful Expressions

Study the bold-faced expressions that are often used in the methodological descriptions of journal articles.

A. Stating the Purpose

- **To effectively incorporate** the motion information in video analysis, we propose to perform 3D convolution in the convolutional layers of CNNs so that discriminative features along both the spatial and the temporal dimensions are captured.
- **In an effort to** drive mobility of solution-processed polymer semiconductors to significantly beyond the current levels, we had focused our investigation on conjugated alternating electron donor2acceptor (D2A) polymers.
- However, **in order to** understand the effects of quenching, we must also consider the growth in stellar mass of non-quenched star-forming galaxies through star formation.
- **To test this hypothesis**, we performed real-time surface plasmon resonance (SPR) assays.
- **To determine** whether PTEN mutations are present in primary tumors, we screened genomic DNA from 18 primary glioblastomas for mutations in three exons.
- **In the interest of** open science, we made our code and data freely available on the Open Science Framework, and our code is additionally available on GitHub.
- There were six behavior items that were included **for the purpose of** further validating the newly developed instrument.

B. Describing the Process

- **The next logical step is to** assess the 3D information of these features **to begin the process of** enhanced image analysis and interpretation under the augmented representation.
- **Before** investigating whether Elg1 promotes RTS1-induced recombination by catalyzing PCNA unloading, we first wanted to confirm that Elg1 is required

- for PCNA unloading in fission yeast.
- A reference electrode (5.08 cm diameter Dermatrode HE-R; American Imex, Irvine, CA, U.S.A.) was placed over the 7th cervical vertebrae **during data collection**.
- **Prior to** analysis, all the turbidity, conductivity, and river level data were quality controlled and assured following standard procedures as per the laboratory data.
- **After** the database search, we identified a total of 422 articles PubMed (n = 120), Embase (n = 147), and WOS (n = 155) and removed the 100 duplicate articles.
- The default keyboard layout was used **in the follow-up phase** for all four subjects.
- The mixture of DM+CM+RS was then selected **for follow-up studies**.
- Safety assessments were done at baseline, **then** every three weeks for the first three months, and **then** every six weeks **thereafter until** treatment was completed or discontinued in the metronomic capecitabine group; **a follow-up visit** was required at one month after discontinuation of treatment.

C. Explaining the Rationale for a Procedure

- **Based on** the outer edge of these two matrix proteins, we divide the PCM into an "inner" and "outer" sphere.
- **On the basis of** neurobehavioral and neurophysiological evidence in patients with cerebellar lesions, it was hypothesized that the cerebellum would influence the speed and accuracy of such attention changes.
- **In light of this**, we aimed to gather as many participants as we could within a limited time window in order to maximize power.

D. Describing the Characteristics of the Sample

- Finally, **it should be noted that** the zCOSMOS-bright sample is **a luminosity-selected sample** and that the stellar mass completeness of the sample therefore **depends quite strongly on** both the redshifts and the range of mass-to-light ratios at the survey limit, i.e., on the galaxy SEDs.
- 74,741(10.0%) participants younger than 18 years or older than 69 years **were excluded** because these age ranges were not considered in the 2004 survey.
- **The samples were subjected to** SDS-PAGE and autoradiography.

- In this method, a dictionary **is first obtained by** training **the samples selected from** the ground-truth data.
- Patients **were sampled without gender or age preference unless indicated.**
- They **include** 17 pieces from four different screen walls of the Hancheng Confucian Temple and 16 samples from four different screen walls of the Town God's Temple. The glazed tile samples **cover** all glaze colors, namely green, yellow, brown, and turquoise.

Part III
Learning Ways of Organization

In this part, we are going to discuss the structures of the Methods sections so as to develop the skills of writing methodological descriptions of academic papers in science and technology.

Serving as the bridge between the literature review and the Results section, the Methods section is informative in nature and includes procedural details in conducting the study. It is an essential part of the research article, particularly for the reporting empirical research. Based on a corpus of 900 journal articles representative of 30 academic fields including 8 arts and humanities, disciplines and 22 natural and applied sciences disciplines, Cotos, Huffman, & Link (2017) proposed a comprehensive cross-disciplinary model of the Methods section, which consists of 3 moves and 16 steps. Examples from different articles are provided to illustrate each step. It should be noted that these moves and steps are functional descriptors instead of an organizational sequence. That is, the order of the moves and steps are not fixed and not all the steps can be found in a single section of methodological descriptions. Choice of steps may vary from discipline to discipline and depend on the nature of the study.

Move 1　Contextualizing Study Methods

Step 1: Referencing Previous Works

e.g., To identify the substrates of Caspase 8, we transcribed and translated in vitro a small pool mouse spleen cDNA library in the presence of 35S-methionine, using the methods of Lustig et al. (1997).

Step 2: Providing General Information

e.g., Solution-processable or printable organic semiconductors have been extensively explored for use in printing organic thin-film transistor (OTFT) arrays and circuits for novel electronic applications.

Step 3: Identifying the Methodological Approach

e.g., Our method, named scDEC, was based on learning a pair of generative adversarial networks (GANs).

Step 4: Describing the Setting

e.g., The study area was located in the Tieqiaoshan Nature Reserve, Shanxi Province, China (Figure 1). The total area of the reserve is 353.52 km^2. This reserve is the most active area in the entire North China leopard distribution area. The reserve contains 39 villages, and the government allows grazing in the reserve in order to increase the incomes of the villagers. The population of the North China leopard in the reserve is always facing the problem of human-wildlife conflict. The highest altitude is 1,827 m, mostly between 1,400 m and 1,700 m. The area has a temperate continental monsoon climate, of alpine and humid type, with an average annual temperature of 6.3℃. The annual precipitation is 593 mm, mainly concentrated in summer in July and August. The North China leopard's common prey are mainly wild boar, roe deer, hare, and pheasant.

Step 5: Introducing the Subjects/Participants

e.g., After exclusions, 645,223 participants aged 18–69 years remained for the present analyses.

Step 6: Rationalizing Pre-experiment Decisions

e.g., BD cases were aggregated into weekly time series format for data analysis. All BD cases were confirmed according to the China National Diagnostic Criteria (WS 287–2008) (National Health and Family Planning Commission [NHFPC], 2008).

Unit 3 Methodological Descriptions

Move 2 Describing the Study

Step 1: Acquiring the Data

e.g., Laser beam shaping through a spatial light modulator and depth-dependent pulse energy compensation are applied to obtain uniform lattices.

Step 2: Describing the Data

e.g., The TRECVID 2008 development data set consists of 49-hour videos captured at London Gatwick Airport using five different cameras with a resolution of 720×576 at 25 fps.

Step 3: Describing Experimental/Study Procedures

e.g., Here we introduce such a simple and green but very efficient and industrially scalable approach (Fig. 1a) using two standard industry steps including: (1) in-situ hydrothermal polymerization/carbonization of the mixture of cheap biomass or industry carbon sources with graphene oxide (GO) to firstly get the 3D hybrid precursor materials and then (2) a chemical activation step to achieve the desired SSA and conductivity. It is important to note that the carbon atom yield is almost 100% from the first step (2), which is a significant and important improvement compared to the conventional direct carbonization process used in the industry due to both the cost and environmental issues.

Step 4: Describing Tools

e.g., Randomization was done with a computer-generated sequence (block size of four), stratified by trial center and receipt of induction chemotherapy (yes or no).

Step 5: Identifying Variables

e.g., Let the independent variable be X_i and the dependent variable be Y_i, the q value acquired from the differentiation and factor detection can be used to measure the heterogeneity of Y_i, and to what extent X_i explains the heterogeneity of Y_i.

Step 6: Rationalizing Experiment Decisions

e.g., The physical significance of maximizing the criterion in Algorithm (2) is to find a projection direction X, onto which all samples are projected, so that the total scatter of the resulting projected samples is maximized.

Step 7: Reporting Incrementals

e.g., The observed mobility was at least an order of magnitude higher than the values of about 1 $cm^2V^{-1}s^{-1}$ recently reported and one to two orders of magnitude higher than those of a-Si: H[6].

Move 3   Establishing Credibility

Step 1: Preparing the Data

e.g., The first step is "Raw Data and Preprocessing". (1) Develop a complete raw data table based on the data released by the involved statistical websites; (2) discrete the continuous data of the independent variables using Python, and divide the 129 Silk Road cities into 10 categories by natural breaks to eliminate artificial influence. If none of the 10 schemes meet the requirements, for example, there is only one city in a given category; the 11th data discretization will be performed with the mean value as the criterion

Step 2: Describing the Data Analysis

e.g., We did student's *t* test for trends for each characteristic in Table 1 and Welch's *t* test for comparisons of mean between groups and over time, and to compare trends in mean BMI before and after 2010.

Step 3: Rationalizing Data Processing/Analysis

e.g., We aggregated and transformed the item responses to a linear scale that ranged from 0 to 100, according to the EORTC scoring manual, in which a higher score represented greater symptom severity (on symptom domains), or a better health status (on the global health status or QOL domain) or function (on functioning domains).

In the following Methods section in an article from *Nature Photonics*, we can see how the move structure is applied.

① The word "fractal" was coined by Mandelbrot for the description of complex structures that usually exhibit self-similarity and non-integer dimension. ② Closely related to humankind, nature, and science, fractality is not only widely embodied in common objects or scenarios, such as branching trees, fluctuations in the stock market, or human heartbeat dynamics, but is also reflected in subtle physical properties and phenomena, such as an energy spectrum or the growth of copper electrodeposits, thereby involving the fields of physiology, finance, quantum mechanics, optics, and so on. ③ Inspired by these natural manifestations, the concept of the fractal has triggered novel designs of materials, photovoltaic and plasmonic devices, enriching the means of material property modification or of artificial device engineering.

④ The role of fractality has been extensively studied in the context of classical transport or diffusion by investigating classical random walks in fractal lattices. ⑤ Alexander and Orbach proposed that the spectral dimension and the Hausdorff dimension govern the classical diffusion in fractals. ⑥ Despite some disagreements on the nature of the diffusion laws, it is beyond doubt that fractality leads to anomalous diffusion, distinctive from regular lattices, in which the mean square displacement (MSD) scales linearly. ⑦ However, the interplay between quantum transport and fractality is still waiting for experimental exploration, despite abundant theoretical studies at non-integer dimensions and pioneering experiments in integer-dimensional ordered, disordered, and non-Hermitian lattices. ⑧ Molecular synthesis, atomic manipulation techniques, and photorefractive materials allow the construction of well-defined fractal structures, but these platforms are not prone to the detection of dynamical properties. ⑨ Photonic lattices based on femtosecond-laser direct-writing techniques, on the other hand, are shown to be the ideal system to investigate quantum-transport dynamics, since they enable the precise design and fabrication of three-dimensional structures.

⑩ Here, we experimentally investigate quantum transport in fractal networks via continuous-time quantum walks of single photons, which are implemented on photonic lattices with identical fractal geometry but incremental propagation lengths. ⑪ With the propagation length increasing, the evolution of photons at different moments is probed, visually revealing the transport dynamics. ⑫ Based on the probability distribution of the evolution patterns, we calculate the MSD and the Pólya number to characterize the transport process. ⑬ Three kinds of fractals are experimentally realized to study the interplay between quantum transport and the geometrical or fractal features of the networks.

(Adapted from "Quantum Transport in Fractal Networks" by X. Xu et al. in *Nature Photonics*, 15, 2021.)

The first two paragraphs in this Methods section (Sentences ①–⑨) function as Move 1 (Contextualizing Study Methods). In this move, the authors provide general information (Move 1, Step 2) by introducing the concept of "fractal" (Sentences ①–③). The authors then refer to a number of studies to situate the method in previous research (Move 1, Step 1), indicating the rationale in the choice of this method (Sentences ④–⑧). In this step, the authors also point out limitations of previous research and unsolved problems (Sentences ⑦–⑧), as in the expressions "However, …is still waiting for experimental exploration", "but these platforms are not prone to the detection of dynamical properties". In light of these limitations and problems, Sentence ⑨ identifies the methodological approach to be used in the current study (Move 1, Step 3) —"Photonic lattices based on femtosecond-laser direct-writing techniques". Sentences ⑩–⑪ then describe experimental procedures (Move 2, Step 3), and Sentences ⑫–⑬ describe the data analysis (Move 3, Step 2).

In this example, emphasis is put on Move 1 (Contextualizing Study Methods). Providing the general information and reviewing previous works can help readers understand why the method used in the current study is chosen and how it is performed. In medical research articles, the Methods section may focus more on Move 2 (Describing the Study) by providing detailed information of data collection and experimental procedures. As said, the choice of the sequence and inclusion of the steps depend largely on the nature of the study and the expectation of the readers in related disciplines. However, there are still some general tips that may apply to all disciplines for writing the methodological descriptions:

- The Methods section should describe the materials used and their functions in enough detail so others can replicate.
- A copy of the materials can be included in an appendix at the end of the paper; you would refer your readers to that appendix (e.g., see Appendix for a complete list of the tools/materials used in this experiment).
- The procedure is like the instructions in recipe for baking a cake. It describes exactly what was done in the study and the order in which things were done.
- The instructions or treatments given to participants (e.g., in a medical experiment) should be described in the Methods section.
- The procedure should be logical, and contain sufficient information for readers to follow.

- The language of this section should be direct and precise. The past tense is mostly used in describing the procedures as the study has been completed at the time of writing the research article.
- The passive voice is often used to maintain an objective tone in the methodological descriptions of research articles in science and technology. However, the choice of the active or passive voice in the Methods section varies from discipline to discipline, and even from journal to journal. It is advisable to follow the conventions of the target journal in your discipline.

In some journals, such as *Nature Medicine* and *Cell*, the methodological descriptions are included in the Results section. In some other journals, such as *The Astrophysical Journal*, the Methods section is labeled as "Experimental Considerations".

Part IV
Analyzing the Examples

In this part, we are going to analyze some examples so as to understand the wording, structures, and moves of methodological descriptions of academic papers in science and technology.

I. **Analyze the following Methods section and discuss the questions with a partner.**

3. Methods

   3.1 Subset Classification of Dataset Catalog

   ① The TCM electronic medical records are electronic files used in TCM hospitals to meet the special needs of TCM clinical diagnoses and treatments as well as for medical management. ② The subset classification of a basic dataset should conform to the TCM electronic medical records business norm, and also address practical application needs, and it should seamlessly relate to and extract the relevant activity records of business information field. ③ Meanwhile, it should maintain certain degree of flexibility and scalability. ④ A thorough research was conducted to examine the data structure and data storage mechanism of the patient diagnoses and treatments business systems, including the TCM electronic medical records system, clinical research and information sharing system, image archiving and communication system, laboratory information system, and hospital information system. ⑤ An outpatient clinical information model and inpatient clinical information model, as shown in Figs. 2 and 3, respectively were then created according to the said subset classification principle. ⑥ The models are built based on the diagnosis and treatment process for patients. ⑦ Here is how the TCM subsets of the datasets are created. ⑧ The TCM electronic medical records are compared against all the seventeen parts of WS 445-2014 standard. ⑨ Based on the two proposed models, a new subset was created where there is a discrepancy between the dataset and the existing standard. ⑩ For example, the subset of acupuncture treatment record, the subset of sticking acupuncture points treatment record, the subset of TCM fumigation and washing treatment record, and the subset of Chinese medicine appropriate technology treatment record are added to Part 5, General Therapy and Treatment Records.

3.2 Selection of Data Element (Metadata)

⑪ The data element, aka metadata, is the smallest unit of electronic medical record data standardization for TCM, and it is also a component of the basic dataset of electronic medical record for TCM. ⑫ The data element is a data unit that uses a set of attributes to describe the definition, identification, representation and allow able value in the context of electronic medical record for TCM. ⑬ The selection of date elements used the bottom-up method based on the 170 thousand patient medical records since 2005. ⑭ To carry out the research, a data traceability system of electronic medical record for TCM was made to analyze the data stored in the database of electronic medical record system. ⑮ First of all, data items were extracted according to the data structure and data storage contents of the electronic medical record, which shows traditional Chinese medicine characteristics, such as "four diagnostic information of TCM", "prescription of TCM", "diagnosis of TCM", "therapeutic principle of TCM", "syndrome differentiation of TCM", "disease of TCM". ⑯ Secondly, the selected data items are analyzed and summarized to be the data element in the basic dataset of electronic medical record of TCM. ⑰ The complex data item that is not easy to parse or cannot accurately express the original data item after parsing can be included in the dataset, such as "syndrome differentiation of TCM". ⑱ If the complex data item can be parsed to a number of data units and every data unit can accurately express the contents of the complex data item, then every parsed data item can be included as data element of the basic dataset. ⑲ For example, "four diagnostic information of TCM" can be parsed and described by "facial expression of inspection diagnosis of TCM", "tongue manifestation of inspection diagnosis of TCM", "breathing condition of auscultation and olfaction diagnosis of TCM", "stool condition of inquiry diagnosis of TCM", "urine condition of inquiry diagnosis of TCM", "pulse condition of pulse-taking diagnosis of TCM", etc. ⑳ Finally, by the data traceability system of electronic medical record for TCM, the data item can be retrieved the frequency of emergence in the electronic medical record for TCM. ㉑ And the universality and suitability of the data element in the basic dataset of electronic medical record for TCM can be verified.

(Adapted from "On Standardization of Basic Datasets of Electronic Medical Records in Traditional Chinese Medicine" by H. Zhang et al. in *Computer Methods and Programs in Biomedicine*, *174*, 2019.)

 Questions:

1. Which sentences indicate Move 1, Move 2, and Move 3 respectively? Can you identify some steps in each move?

2. What tenses and voices are used in the Methods section? Why are they used?

II. Analyze the following Materials and Methods section and discuss the questions with a partner.

Substrate Characteristics

① DM and CM were collected from a livestock farm located in Yangling, China. RS was obtained from a local villager. Before being put into the reactor, the air-dried RS was cut into pieces. ② The substrates were individually homogenized and subsequently stored at 4uC for further use. ③ The chemical characterization of each substrate tested in this study is shown in Table 1. ④ All samples were collected and tested in triplicate, and the averages of the three measurements are presented.

Experimental Design and Set-up

⑤ Experiment 1: Three mixture sets were investigated in this experiment: set A (DM+RS), set B (CM+RS), and set C (DM+CM+RS). ⑥ For set A and set B, the C/N ratio was 25, achieved by adjusting the DM/RS or CM/RS ratio. For set C, based on a DM/CM ratio of 1:1, multi-component substrates were prepared by adding RS to the DM-CM mixtures in order to adjust the C/N ratio to 25. ⑦ The proportions of all substrates in each mixture were in a volatile solid (VS) state. ⑧ The operation temperatures were 20, 30, 40 (mesophilic), 50, and 60 uC (thermophilic), respectively.

Experiment 2: (Omitted)

...

⑨ The initial VS ratio of substrate to inoculum was kept at 1:2 for all experimental set-ups. ⑩ Each reactor had a 1 L capacity and contained 600 mL of total liquid, including 200 mL of inoculum and mixed substrate of 15 gVS/L. ⑪ The inoculum used for digestion at 20, 30, 35, and 40 uC was digested cattle manure, taken from a lab-scale reactor operated at 35 uC with a hydraulic retention time (HRT) of 15 days. ⑫ Additionally, digestion at 50, 55, and 60 uC was inoculated with digested cattle manure from the lab-scale reactor operated at 55 uC with a HRT of 15 days. ⑬ A control with only inoculum was used to determine biogas production due to endogenous respiration. ⑭ Each treatment was performed in triplicate. ⑮ All reactors were tightly closed with rubber septa and screw caps. ⑯ The headspace of each reactor was flushed with nitrogen gas for about three minutes to assure anaerobic conditions prior to starting the digestion tests. ⑰ To provide mixing of the reactor contents, all reactors were shaken manually for about one minute, once a day prior to measurement of biogas volume.

Analytical Techniques

⑱ Total solids, VS, pH, Total Kjeldahl Nitrogen (TKN) and total ammonium nitrogen (TAN) analysis were performed according to APHA Standard Methods. ⑲ Total organic carbon was determined by the method described by Cuetos et al. ⑳ For all treatments, FA concentration was calculated in accordance with Hansen et al. ㉑ The volume of biogas was measured by displacement of water. ㉒ Methane content in the produced biogas was analyzed with a fast methane analyzer (Model DLGA-1000, Infrared Analyzer, Dafang, Beijing, China). ㉓ The C/N ratio was determined by dividing the total organic carbon content by the total nitrogen content, according to the following equation.

$$C = N\text{\textasciitilde}W1|C1zW2|C2zW3|C3\ W1|N1zW2|N2zW3|N3$$

(Adapted from "Effects of Temperature and Carbon-nitrogen (C/N) Ratio on the Performance of Anaerobic Co-digestion of Dairy Manure, Chicken Manure and Rice Straw: Focusing on Ammonia Inhibition" by X. Wang et al. in *PLOS One*, 9(5), 2014.)

 Questions:

1. Which sentences describe the setting of the study?

2. What are the materials used in the study?

3. Which sentences list the procedures of the study?

III. **Analyze the following Materials and Methods section and discuss the questions with a partner.**

2. Materials and Methods

2.1 Sample Information

Thirty-three fragments of glazed tiles traced back to several different periods of the Ming and Qing Dynasties (ca. 1482–1722 AD) were collected in this study. They include 17 pieces from four different screen walls of the Hancheng Confucian Temple and 16 samples from four different screen walls of the Town God's Temple. The glazed tile samples cover all glaze colors, namely green, yellow, brown, and turquoise. Details are shown in Table 1. The appearances of some typical samples are shown in Figure 5.

2.2 Analytical Methods

2.2.1 Scanning Electron Microscopy (SEM) with Energy Dispersive Spectroscopy (EDS)

A Zeiss instrument, model EVO-250 SEM (Zeiss, the instrument is located in Xi'an, China), coupled with an Oxford Instruments X-MAX20 EDS system, was used to study the samples' microstructure and the body and glaze compositions. A cross-section of each representative sample was taken off and mounted as a polished block. The acceleration voltage used for observation and analysis was 20 keV with a working distance of 8 mm. SEM backscattered electron (BSE) images of the microstructure of the body paste and glaze were recorded. For each sample, the chemical compositions of the tile body and glaze were analyzed in three micro areas and the average values were calculated. The size analyzed by EDS both for the body and the glaze is around 200~300 um. The test time of EDS was 90 s. Oxford Instruments standards were used to quantify 10 elements (Si, Al, Na, K, Mg, Ca, and Fe for the tile body, while Pb, Si, Al, Na, K, Mg, Ca, Fe, Cu, and Ti for the tile glaze). The results were converted into oxide percentages and normalized to 100%. The detection limit of the instrument is 0.1%. The glaze chemical compositions of all 33 samples have been analyzed in this study. For the chemical compositions of paste, only 23 samples (C1–10 and T1–13) have been analyzed. The reason is that the pastes of samples C11–17 and samples T14–16 have already decayed heavily, so the pastes of these samples look loose and fragile (having suffered from salt efflorescence); therefore, if these samples were tested for their chemical compositions, inaccurate results would be obtained.

2.2.2 X-ray Diffraction (XRD)

Eighteen tile bodies of the samples and two samples of solute salt powder were tested by XRD (Rigaku SmartLab) for their phase analysis. Before the test, a small amount of the tile body of each sample was taken off and ground into fine powder. A 2θ range of 5–55° was used, with the detector type being a D/teX Ultra 250 silicon strip detector device (SmartLab, the instrument is located in Xi'an, China). A tube voltage of 30 kV with a current of 300 mA was applied.

2.2.3 Analytical Methods for Degradation Process

To discuss body salt efflorescence, a glazed tile sample (T-15) with intact glaze but weathered-looking paste was scanned by a micro-CT scanner (NanoVoxel 3000, the instrument is located in Tianjing, China) with 190 keV voltage, and a 25W-power was used on the X-ray source. Sequences of grayscale images were obtained, which can be reconstructed into a 3D image. The image resolution is 0.5 um per voxel length.

The moisture contents at different heights (25 to 250 cm from the ground with 25 cm as the measurement interval) of five screen walls have been tested with the HF

Unit 3　Methodological Descriptions

SENSOR MOIST 210 non-destructive moisture measurer (HF SENSOR, the instrument is located in Xi'an, China). Due to the fact that variances in the moisture content at different depths of the screen wall also need to be compared, the areas for the test were measured at the gray brick zone to ensure consistency.

(Adapted from "Architectural Glazed Tiles Used in Ancient Chinese Screen Walls (15th–18th Century AD): Ceramic Technology, Decay Process and Conservation" by J. Shen et al. in *Materials*, *14*(23), 2021.)

 Questions:

1. Can you underline the expressions that describe the characteristics of the samples?

2. Underline the sentences in Section 2.2.1 that rationalize pre-experiment decisions.

3. What are the steps in the process of XRD described in Section 2.2.2?

4. Underline the sentence in Section 2.2.3 that indicates the purpose of using a particular analytical method.

Exercises

I. Read the following Materials and Methods section and put the number of sentences into the right cells of the table.

4. Materials and Methods

4.1. Participants and Procedure

① The participants were recruited in an online self-report study conducted in Poland in 2021. ② Only workers interacting with cobots on a daily basis took part in the survey. ③ Participation in the study was voluntary. ④ The respondents did not receive any compensation for participation. ⑤ The institutional ethics committee of the University of Silesia in Katowice approved the project of this research (decision number KEUS 125/05.2021). ⑥ The study was conducted according to the principles of the Declaration of Helsinki.

⑦ The sample in the study comprised 190 cobot operators, of whom 114 (60%) were men and 76 (40%) were women. ⑧ The participants ranged in age from 23 to 55 years ($M = 37.95$, $SD = 6.53$). ⑨ The majority of participants (91.1%) had higher education, 8.4% had upper secondary education, and 0.5% had primary education. ⑩ The participants' seniority in working with robots ranged from 3 months to 35 years ($M = 6.46$, $SD = 5.56$).

⑪ The operators collaborated with several types of cobots, including Kuka (BR iiwa 7 R800 and R800 CR, LBR iiwa 15 R820), FANUC (CR-4iA and CR-7iA, CR-7iA/L and CR-14iA/L, CRX-10iA and CRX-10iA/L, CR-15iA and CR-35iA), Universal Robots (UR3/UR3e, UR5/UR5e, UR10/UR10e), ABB (Yumi), Kawasaki (duAro), ALVO Ultra V-bot, Mitsubishi (MELFA Assista), Yaskawa (MOTOMAN HC20DT), OMRON Collaborative Robot, and Epson Collaborative Robot.

4.2. Measures

Fluency in Human-robot Interaction Scale

⑫ The scale created by Paliga (2021) was adapted to measure HRI fluency. ⑬ The original scale comprises six items and allows measuring three perspectives of human-robot interaction (two items each): the human-, the robot-, and the team-oriented perspective on a seven-point Likert scale (1 = *I strongly disagree* to 7 = *I strongly agree*). ⑭ In this study, two changes in the scale were made. ⑮ First, three items indicating the theoretically based human contribution-oriented perspective were added. ⑯ Second, in order to make the subscales stronger and more stable, each subscale was supplemented with one additional item sourced from Hoffman & Breazeal (2007a, 2007b) and Hoffman (2019). ⑰ This resulted in a 12-item scale to measure four latent factors of HRI fluency (three items each). ⑱ To confirm the structure of the scale, confirmatory factor analysis was applied. ⑲ The results (χ^2 = 64.59; df = 50; *p* = .08; RMSEA = .04; 95% CI = .001–.06; CFI = .99; NFI=.97; SRMR = .02) proved that the four-dimensional model of HRI fluency fit the data well. ⑳ All factor loadings were above .72. ㉑ Table 1 shows the items used in the extended version of Fluency in Human-robot Interaction Scale and Cronbach's alphas for each subscale. ㉒ All Cronbach's alphas are above .83, which indicates the goodness of the scale for idiographic assessment.

Job Performance

㉓ Job performance was measured using three items from Williams and Anderson's (1991) instrument (e.g., "I perform tasks that are expected of me"). ㉔ The participants used a seven-point Likert scale (1 = *I strongly disagree* to 7 = *I strongly agree*) to indicate their answer regarding performance during work with the cobot. ㉕ Cronbach's α was .87.

Work Engagement

㉖ The 9-items Utrecht Work Engagement Scale (UWES-9) was used to assess the level of employees' unidimensional engagement in work with a cobot (e.g., "At my work, I feel bursting with energy"). ㉗ The items were scored on a 7-point Likert scale ranging from 0 (never) to 6 (every day). ㉘ Cronbach's α for the total score was .96.

(Adapted from "Human-cobot Interaction Fluency and Cobot Operators' Job Performance. The Mediating Role of Work Engagement: A Survey" by M. Paliga in *Robotics and Autonomous Systems*, 155, 2022.)

Moves	Sentence Number(s)
Move 1: Contextualizing Study Methods	
Move 2: Describing the Study	
Move 3: Establishing Credibility	

II. Read the following paragraphs taken from the Methods section and fill in the blanks with appropriate verb forms.

Thermal infrared (TIR) images (1) _____ (capture) using the Thermal Capture Fusion Zoom camera. The camera (2) _____ (contain) a thermal FLIR Tau 2 core with a thermal resolution of 0.05 K and (3) _____ (record) GPS positions. Image data with a spatial resolution of 640×512 pixels (4) _____ (collect) with 9 Hz frequency. Conversion of digital numbers (DN) to brightness temperature (BT) was carried out in TeAx Thermo viewer (5) _____ (use) an assumed emissivity of 1. Raw images (6) _____ (select) to have 80% front overlap and were subjected to a photogrammetric processing workflow using Agisoft Metashape. Canopy temperatures (Tc) were retrieved from BT according to the two-step process (7) _____ (describe) in Heinemann et al. (2020). First land surface emissivity (LSE) maps (8) _____ (derive) from NDVI and then the derived LSE used to calculate Tc. Accuracy of the retrieved Tc from the drone data, (9) _____ (verify) against ground thermometers at positions of IRT sensors (IR 1–6; Fig. 1), after extraction of "pure" image Tc using NDVI masking (Zhang et al., 2019). Results (10) _____ (give) an R^2 value of 0.71 and RMSE of 2.1 ℃.

(Adapted from "Revisiting Crop Water Stress Index Based on Potato Field Experiments in Northern Germany" by E. K. Ekinzog et al. in *Agricultural Water Management, 269*, 2022.)

III. Rewrite the following sentences using the passive voice or active voice. Then discuss with your partner which tense would be more appropriate for each sentence.

(1) We designed a library including commensal, pathogenic, and probiotic bacterial species as well as positive and negative controls.

_____

_____

Unit 3　**Methodological Descriptions**

(2) Here, we report a lead halide-templated crystallization strategy to prepare compact methylamine-free perovskite films for the fabrication of antisolvent-free and ambient air-printed high-performance PSMs.

_____

_____

(3) In order to prepare reactant N_2^+ ions in the ground electronic state with the internal vibrational excitation of $v^+ = 0$, 1, or 2 by using the single-photon VUV-PFI-PI technique, the VUV laser radiation generated by the resonance-enhanced four-wave frequency mixing scheme in Kr gas as the non-linear medium is adopted.

_____

_____

(4) In this multicenter, randomized, open-label, blinded-outcome trial in Europe and Canada, we recruited patients with stroke due to large vessel occlusion confirmed with CT or magnetic resonance angiography admitted to endovascular centers.

_____

_____

(5) Based on the results obtained, the influence of defects in the material structure on the stress and strain distribution was analyzed.

_____

_____

IV. The following sentences come from the Methods section of an academic paper and are in scrambled order. Rearrange them to make a coherent paragraph.

　A. Coordinates of the first color change detected alone the ray are recorded as a point *P* of the inner contour of the copper deposit.

　B. In order to measure the deposit thickness, the perpendicular distance to the mandrel from point *P* to the outer contour is constructed.

C. The distance between this intersection and point *P* is considered as the deposit thickness.

D. To determine the coordinates of the center of rotation of the mandrel, the coordinates of the centroid (determined with the built-in MATLAB function "regionprops" from the Image toolbox) of the through-hole left in the mandrel after shaft removal were used.

E. A ray originating from the mandrel's center of rotation (centroid of the through-hole left by the shaft) at an angle α with the *x*-axis was constructed.

F. A line perpendicular to the tangent line of the osculating circle and passing through point *P* has an intersection with the outer contour of the deposition.

G. Afterward, to determine the thickness of the deposits, images were first converted into binary pictures.

H. Therefore, the osculating circle to the mandrel at point *P* is determined using two adjacent points to *P*.

(Adapted from "Towards Electroforming of Copper Net-shape Parts on Fused Deposition Modeling (FDM) Printed Mandrels" by Z. Zheng et al in *The International Journal of Advanced Manufacturing Technology*, 2022.)

Order: _____

📝 Project

Work in groups. Choose 3–4 journal articles from different authoritative international journals in your discipline and discuss the wording, style, and organization of the methodological descriptions. Prepare a presentation to be delivered in class.

Unit 4

Results and Discussions

Part I
Introducing the Unit

The Results section of a research article answers the research questions by reporting the findings of a study. It usually goes right after the methodological descriptions. In contrast, the Discussion section interprets the results and discusses the contribution of the study to the field of research. Therefore, the Results section is more descriptive, mainly driven by facts, while the Discussion section is more interpretative, mainly driven by opinions. It is, however, sometimes difficult to separate the Discussion section from the Results section. Different arrangements of these two sections can be found in journal articles. Some writers combine their results and discussion in one section, while others discuss the results in a separate section or include the discussion in the Conclusion section.

In this unit, we are going to learn about the structures, contents, and language uses of the results and discussions of research articles and how to report and interpret them in a proper way.

After finishing this unit, you are expected to achieve the following learning objectives:

- to understand the differences between the Results and Discussion sections in research articles;
- to acquire the organizational patterns and rhetorical moves in the Results and Discussion sections in research articles;
- to use signal phrases and typical expressions in writing the Results and Discussion sections;
- to learn how to report and discuss results in research articles in your discipline.

Part II
Learning Useful Expressions

Study the bold-faced expressions that are often used in the results and discussions of journal articles.

A. Hedging (Softening) a Claim

- This **may** be due to the fact that wild boars **are more likely to** be distributed on the edge of the forest and even feed on crops, while roe deer are more afraid of people and avoid human interference.
- Substrates that have low C/N ratios contain relatively high concentrations of ammonia, exceeding concentrations necessary for microbial growth, and **probably** inhibiting anaerobic digestion.
- The signature we observed is also very similar to that of the blue pigment used in early Islamic glazed ceramics, **suggesting** that the cobalt ores from the Anarak mining district, rather than those originating from Qamsar, Kashan as previously thought, **might** have served as one of **the most likely** sources of the imported pigment used for Chinese imperial blue-and-white porcelains.
- Among them, a group of so-called "BH3-only" death agonists, including Bik/Bbk, BID, Hrk/DP5, and newly identified Blk, **seem to** be more potent than other death agonists in the family that contains additional BH1 and BH2 domains such as BAD.
- In addition, there are some other **possible reasons** for the above phenomena, such as the insufficient number of samples, the lack of pre-training for the categories in the feature extractor, and so no.

B. Boosting (Strengthening) a Claim

- The backscatter images (Fig. 4) **clearly demonstrate** massive high brightness residual pigment particles in the blue regions, and the morphology and distribution of these particles present certain patterns.
- Additionally, the moisture content of the surface area (d = 2–3 cm) is **evidently** higher than that of the interior area (d = 25–30 cm).
- Specifically, we see small changes in the M* and as for the dominant population of passive galaxies in D4 relative to D1 that are consistent with

- the effects of a small amount (Δm~15% and **definitely** less than 40%) of subsequent dry merging in D4.
- The slight disagreement between the experiment and the simulation is due to **inevitable** imperfections in practical fabrications and realistic experimental environments, especially for such a large-scale lattice.

Useful Expressions in the Results Section

A. Locating Information in Tables or Figures

- A comparison of 2D and 3D convolutions **is given in Fig. 1**.
- The results of the experiment **are shown in Fig. 6**, where **Fig. 6a, b, and c shows** the relation diagram between the number of DRs and the phase shift of the meta-atoms at 0.265 THz, 0.260 THz, and 0.270 THz, respectively.
- **As observed in Fig. 2**, the first subimage contains most of the energy of the original image.
- **Table 2 indicates** that feature extraction by 2DPCA takes much less time.
- Unlike the previous works (**see Table I**), there is still no open work to survey the RA problems of HetNets.
- The horizontal lines again show the fits to functions of the form of Equation (5), **with the values given in Table 2**.

B. Making Comparisons

- And the conductivities of these products (~102 S/m) are not only about **two orders higher than** that of RP20 (~5 S/m) at the pristine state, and even **significantly higher than** that (~47 S/m) of RP20 mixed with 10% of conductive carbon black (CB).
- In most cases, the NMM **is superior to** the LMM, in that it can better describe the social interactions occurring at the Earth's surface.
- **Compared with** ammonium nitrogen, FA has been suggested as the active component causing ammonia inhibition, since it is freely membrane-permeable.
- A recent study shows that, **in contrast with** SARS-CoV S, which does not contain furin recognition sites between S1 and S2, SARS-CoV-2 S contains one potential cleavage site and could be efficiently processed into S1 and S2.
- Disorders also increased with age with those over 65 reporting reproductive disorders **five times more likely than** those under 18 years of age.
- **Similar to** other reported betaCoV CTD structures, this protein also exhibits

two structural domains.

- **Similarly**, the frames Fig.9(i)–Fig.9(l) reflect how the vehicle behaved when it met a group of people blocking the way ahead.
- To set an empty matrix Q, the size was **the same as** the number of regions which was generated after field image was divided by window, marked as 40 by 320.
- **In the same way**, at 0.260 THz, a total phase shift of over 30° and an insertion loss of less than 7 dB can be achieved.

C. Stating General Findings

- **Overall**, the experiment results unveil the performance of several state-of-the-art detectors on CDBV, providing baselines for other researches.
- **On the whole**, the research suggests consistently positive results in realms, including ADHD.
- **In general**, open, population, coordination, innovation, and investment are major driving forces determining the size of urban industrial land stock in Silk Road cities, while industry, green, and cost are less influential.
- However, **the overall results** indicate that V2b suppression of motor neuron spiking is not robust.
- **With one exception** (DU145), all of the cell lines retained a mutant PTEN allele and lost the other allele, indicating that these cells are null for PTEN.

Useful Expressions in the Discussion Section

A. Stating Limitations of the Research

- Until further data are available, use of apixaban **should be restricted to** patients at low risk for acute kidney injury: Those who are clinically stable.
- However, **this does not imply that** the eigenvectors can be evaluated accurately in this way since the eigenvectors are statistically determined by the covariance matrix, no matter what method is adopted for obtaining them.
- **Unfortunately, we could not clarify this assumption** as we could not retrieve documentation that clearly.
- **However, the lack of** a reference standard **prevented us from** determining which samples best represented the true structure.
- First, the study was done in an endemic region; therefore, whether the

- findings can be applied to non-endemic areas, such as in Europe and North America, **remains to be elucidated.**
- Third, different induction chemotherapy regimens and cycles were used, **which might introduce potential bias.**

B. Stating Contributions of the Research

- Despite the limitations mentioned above, **the results can provide important insight into** adult behavior relating to environmental health risks.
- This research **enables us to better understand** the raw materials and technological choices used to produce the glazed tiles which decorate ancient Chinese screen walls.
- **The results support a potential role for** adjuvant therapy using metronomic chemotherapy in the treatment of nasopharyngeal carcinoma.
- Although further monitoring is needed to assess the longer-term trends and changing patterns, **the present study findings highlight the pressing need for** more targeted health policies to reduce further increases in obesity in the general population.
- Our practical protocols also **have important implications in the field of** archaeological dating, artwork authentication, and historical vicissitude.
- This phenomenon **not only reveals** an intriguing property of collagen; it **also provides an exciting concept for** enhancing the mechanical properties of hybrid materials through internal stresses similar to concrete that is prestressed by steel fibers.

Part III
Learning Ways of Organization

In this Part, we are going to discuss the structures of the Results and Discussion sections so as to develop the skills of reporting and discussing research results of academic papers in science and technology.

Ways of Organizing the Results Section

The Results section should report the findings of a study in a concise and logical way without bias or interpretation. Before presenting the findings, we should provide the context or background of the study by restating the research purpose or research questions. Annesley (2010) suggests four ways of organizing results depending on the type of research reported: chronological order, grouping by topic or experiment, general to specific, and most to least important. Chronological order is more suitable for studies describing a process or observing changes over time. If the study involves multiple experiments, grouping by topic or experiment can work better than others. We could also report the general findings first to provide an overall picture and then move on to specific details in the Results section. Moreover, we can show the readers the observations that are most relevant to the topic under investigation before reporting less important findings. The length of the Results section should be consistent with the number and type of data collected in the study. Subheadings are necessary for a long Results section, indicating different topics in the section. The example below illustrates the results of a study in the chronological order.

> We describe three aspects that have a strong influence on the mineralization process. First, when using a precursor solution without PAA, no stress generation was observed. In this case no mineral phase was formed inside the fibrils (Fig. 2C and Fig. S3A), which indicated that molecular interactions between collagen and minerals inside fibrils were a prerequisite for contraction. Small $SrCO_3$ particles were nucleated only at the surface of the tendon, as expected for a mineralization process in supersaturated solution (Fig. S6).
>
> Second, tendon samples were immersed into different solutions with the same total concentration of ions, to test whether the interaction with ions or the mineralization process was the origin of the contraction (Fig. S7). No stress generation occurred if only either Sr^{2+} or CO_3^{2-} ions were present in the solution. Stress increased solely if both mineralizing ions (Sr^{2+} and CO_3^{2-}) were present and caused intrafibrillar mineralization. Therefore, the deposition of minerals inside collagen fibrils (intrafibrillar mineralization) plays a dominant role for stress generation. Third, by modifying the pH value of the mineralizing solution, the degree of mineralization could be controlled. A higher pH value of the solution led to a fast increase of stress in the initial stage of tendon mineralization, ranging from 0.03 MPa/hour at a pH of 8.5 to 0.095 MPa/hour at a pH of 9 (inset of Fig. 2A). That

pH influences the rate of stress generation could also indicate a role of collagen charges in the process.

(Adapted from "Mineralization Generates Megapascal Contractile Stresses in Collagen Fibrils" by H. Ping et al. in *Science*, *376*(6589), 2022.)

The excerpt above follows a chronological order, indicated by the words "first" and "second". For a longer Results section, subsections are more helpful for readers, as seen the following outline of the Results section.

Results

Modeling and Simulation Studies

Synthesis, Processing, and Optimization of Semiconductor 1

Physical Characterization

OTFT Fabrication and Characterization

Temperature-dependent and Ambipolar FET Characteristics

Hysteresis, Bias Stress Effects, and Device Stability

Inverters and Circuits

(Adapted from "A Stable Solution-processed Polymer Semiconductor with Record High-mobility for Printed Transistors" by J. Li et al. in *Scientific Reports, 754*, 2012.)

The purpose of the article is to report "the processing and optimization of solution-processable polymer semiconductors for thin-film transistors, demonstrating very high field-effect mobility, high on/off ratio, and excellent shelf-life and operating stabilities under ambient conditions". From the outline above, we can see that the Results section is organized in the way of grouping by topic, starting from the processing of the model and the optimization of the semiconductor, then characteristics from different aspects.

When reporting the results of a study in scientific articles, we often use non-textual elements such as tables, graphs, diagrams, drawings, figures, and flow charts. These non-textual elements are visually engaging and useful in presenting results. Several rules should be kept in mind when reporting results with non-textual elements. Firstly, all these elements must have a clear title that informs readers of the presented information, such as "Figure 1. SARS-CoV-2-S1 and SARS-CoV-2-CTD Co-localize with hACE2" and "Table 1. Absolute Integral Cross Sections ($Å^2$) of the CT and HT Channels of the Vibrationally State-selected Ion-molecule Reaction". Secondly, non-textual elements should be placed as close as possible to the narration of the information presented in these elements. Location statements, such as "Figures 1a–1c show three kinds of typical high crop stubble images captured when they were being tilled", are included in the narration to direct readers to the non-textural elements. Thirdly, non-textual elements should be put in the Appendix part if there are too many of them. Remember, excessive non-textual elements may disrupt the narration and confuse readers.

Ways of Organizing the Discussion Section

The purpose of the Discussion section is to interpret the findings of the study and describe the significance of these findings in relation to what is known on the topic. Based on 252 research articles in seven disciplines, Peacock (2002) put forward an eight-move model for the Discussion section:

- Move 1: Information move (background about theory / research aims / methodology);
- Move 2: Finding (with or without a reference to a graph or table);
- Move 3: Expected or unexpected outcome (comment on whether the results are expected or not);
- Move 4: Reference to previous research;
- Move 5: Explanation (reasons for expected or unexpected results);
- Move 6: Claim (contribution to research [sometimes with recommendations for action]);
- Move 7: Limitation;
- Move 8: Recommendation (suggestions for future research).

The eight moves can be classified in three parts:

- Part I Introduction: Move 1, or 2, or 6.
- Part II Evaluation: The key move cycles are 2+4, 2+6, 3+4, and 3+5. Other less common cycles are 6+4 and 4+6.
- Part III Conclusion: Move(s) 2+6, or 8, or 8+6, or 7+6.

In the Discussion section below, Sentence ① is the information move, restating the research aim of the study—developing a kind of material which can be processed into a semiconductor (Move 1). Sentences ②–④ report the finding of the study (Move 2). Sentence ⑤ and Sentence ⑥ claim the significance and contribution of the study (Move 6), while Sentence ⑦ refers to the previous research by pointing out the deficiency and limitations of existing theory of charge transport in organic systems (Move 4). As seen from the outline of the Results section of this article (provided in the last section), a detailed report of the results has been provided. Compared to the Results section, the Discussion section is more concise, summarizing the major findings while highlighting the significance of the study.

Discussion

① We have developed a very high molecular-weight DPP-DTT-based polymer, which can be solution-processed into an ambient-stable, high-performance thin-film semiconductor for OTFT application. ② OTFT devices fabricated with this polymer semiconductor have exhibited very high mobility (up to 10.5 $cm^2 V^{-1} s^{-1}$) and on/off ratio ($106), together with excellent FET performance characteristics and exceptional device shelf-life and operational stabilities. ③ The temperature-dependent characteristics of the transport behavior of this polymer semiconductor unequivocally attest to a hopping mode transport mechanism with low activation energy. ④ Very high-gain PMOS inverter devices and functional oscillator circuits have been fabricated from this polymer semiconductor, demonstrating its potential for broad-range, high-value technological applications. ⑤ These results represent a significant achievement in organic semiconductor development and are expected to help propel technological translation of printed electronics from laboratory to marketplace. ⑥ From the theoretical perspective, the ability of a polycrystalline polymer semiconductor to achieve a single crystal-like charge carrier transport points to the deficiency and limitations of existing theory of charge transport in organic systems. ⑦ This high-mobility polymer semiconductor will thus be of fundamental importance to organic semiconductor research and organic electronics.

(Adapted from "A Stable Solution-processed Polymer Semiconductor with Record High-mobility for Printed Transistors" by J. Li et al. in *Scientific Reports, 754*, 2012.)

Unit 4　Results and Discussions

It should be noted that the Results and Discussion sections can be combined in some research articles, while being separated in other articles. Or sometimes we may find the Discussion and Conclusion sections are combined. Choice of these options depends on the conventions in the specific discipline and requirements of the target journal. In the following example, the Results and Discussion sections are combined; in each sub-section, the results are reported and discussed.

> 3. Results and Discussion
>
>   3.1 Defect Analysis Based on Micro-CT
>
>   3.2 Stress and Strain Fields in Struts
>
>   3.3 Mechanical Properties
>
> (Adapted from "Numerical Investigation of the Defects Effect in Additive Manufactured Ti-6Al-4V Struts on Deformation Behavior Based on Microtomographic Images" by M. Doroszko in *Materials*, *15*, 2022.)

Part IV
Analyzing the Examples

In this part, we are going to analyze some examples so as to understand the wording, structures, and moves of results and discussions of academic papers in science and technology.

I.　Analyze the following Results section and discuss the questions with a partner.

  ① To measure the effectiveness of the navigation path detection algorithm, 20 images for each high crop stubble field were tested. ② The results showed that almost all the navigation paths overlapped with the corresponding high crop stubble tilled and non-tilled boundaries. ③ The candidate points that extracted from shearing binary image could effectively reflect the tilled and non-tilled boundary information and were nearly not affected by white spots in tilled areas. ④ That was, the algorithm was strong to resist interference. ⑤ The results show that processing time is less than 0.6 s;

therefore, the least square method for fitting navigation path increased detection speed and high precision; hence it was suitable for real-time processing.

⑥ Figures 6a–6c were rice, rape, and wheat high crop stubble field images with big slope tillage boundaries from left to right, captured when tractor was keeping close to tillage boundaries. ⑦ Figures 6d–6f were the corresponding detection results. ⑧ The experiment showed that the algorithm was well adaptive to larger slope navigation path images.

(Adapted from "Automatic Navigation Path Detection Method for Tillage Machines Working on High Crop Stubble Fields Based on Machine Vision" by T. Zhang et al. in *International Journal of Agriculture and Biological Engineering, 7*(4), 2014.)

 Questions:

1. What moves in Peacock's (2002) model can you identify in the excerpt?

2. Which words and expressions show the contribution of the study?

3. Which sentences are location statements that introduce non-textual elements in the excerpt?

II. Analyze the following Results and Discussion sections and discuss the questions with a partner.

Results

Prespecified secondary clinical efficacy outcomes and technical efficacy outcomes are shown in Table 2. At 90 days, 22 (11%) of 201 patients assigned to thrombectomy alone and 17 (8%) of 207 patients assigned to intravenous alteplase plus thrombectomy had died (risk difference 2.3%, 95% CI –3.2 to 7.8, Appendix p 11). There were no significant differences regarding the full distribution of modified Rankin scale scores at 90 days (common odds ratio for a better outcome 0.75, 95% CI 0.53–1.06, $p = 0.10$).

Successful reperfusion before thrombectomy (cross-sectional expanded TICI 2b50–3) occurred in two (1%) of 201 patients assigned to thrombectomy alone and eight (4%) of 207 patients assigned to intravenous alteplase plus thrombectomy

Unit 4 Results and Discussions

(risk difference −2.9%, 95% CI −6.0 to 0.3%, $p = 0.077$). After completion of all endovascular procedures, successful reperfusion was less frequently observed in patients assigned to thrombectomy alone (cross-sectional expanded TICI 2b50–3 in 182 (91%) of 201 vs 199 (96%) of 207, risk difference −5.1%, 95% CI −10.2 to 0.0%, $p = 0.047$). In the complete cohort, only two (7%) of 27 patients in whom reperfusion was not successful (cross-sectional expanded TICI < 2b50) were functionally independent at 90 days.

Discussion

Given the results reported here and the fact that the only other trial evaluating thrombectomy alone in white patients also did not show non-inferiority, omitting intravenous alteplase in this population seems unjustified.

Administration of intravenous alteplase did not increase the risk of symptomatic intracranial haemorrhage, although the statistical power to detect a difference was limited by the small number of symptomatic bleeds. An individual patient data meta-analysis of trials comparing intravenous alteplase with placebo or open control found that intravenous alteplase led to a 5.5% absolute increase in the risk of type 2 parenchymal haemorrhage (6.8% vs 1.3%). Besides power considerations related to study size, the lack of a clear association of intravenous alteplase with increased bleeding risk in this study might also be associated with overall good reperfusion, which seems to protect patients from haemorrhages and haemorrhagic transformations.

Hypothesis-generating subgroup analyses suggested heterogeneity of the comparison of thrombectomy alone versus intravenous alteplase plus thrombectomy with regard to age. In contrast to the overall study results, the treatment effect was close to the null effect in patients aged 70 years or older, but still crossed the non-inferiority margin of 12%. A differential effect of alteplase according to age was not anticipated, as trials comparing intravenous alteplase with placebo did not detect an age-related change in the effect of alteplase on the odds of good outcome. In addition, no other trial found comparable heterogeneity of the relative treatment effect with age strata. Until further evidence becomes available, this observation should be treated with caution, because there is a non-negligible likelihood that the observed heterogeneity is due to chance.

(Adapted from "Thrombectomy Alone Versus Intravenous Alteplase plus Thrombectomy in Patients with Stroke: An Open-label, Blinded-outcome, Randomized Non-inferiority Trial" by U. Fischer et al. in *The Lancet*, 400, 2022.)

 Questions:

1. In what ways do these two sections differ?

2. In what ways are they similar?

3. How is the Results section organized? Chronological order, grouping by topic or experiment, general to specific, or most to least important?

Exercises

I. Which of the following categories is better placed in the Results section and which is better in the Discussion section? Write R for the Results section and D for the Discussion section.

(1) _____ reporting findings (with or without a reference to a graph or table)

(2) _____ citing the agreement or discrepancy with previous studies

(3) _____ restating the research aim

(4) _____ pointing out limitations of current study

(5) _____ providing reasons for expected or unexpected results

(6) _____ telling contribution to the research area

(7) _____ showing expected or unexpected outcomes

(8) _____ making recommendations or suggestions for future research

II. Collect 30 journal articles from your research area and examine the last parts of these articles. They might be labeled in one of the following ways. Fill in the table below and consider which way of the organization is the most common among these articles. Be prepared to discuss your findings with a partner.

Ways of Organization (Labeling)	Number of Articles
Results and Discussion (separate)	
Results and Discussion (combined)	
Results and Conclusions (separate)	
Discussion and Conclusions (combined)	
Results, Discussion, and Conclusions (all separate)	
Summary and Conclusions (separate)	
Summary and Conclusions (combined)	

Ways of Organization (Labeling)	Number of Articles
No label (subtitle) for any of the sections	
Other ways of arrangements	

(Continued)

III. **Rewrite the following sentences using different expressions of making comparison without changing the original meanings.**

(1) For the action class Pointing, the 3D CNN model achieves slightly worse performance than the other three methods.

(2) Based on the plastic strain distributions, it can be seen that the maximum values obtained are about 10 times higher than the nominal strain value.

(3) The recognition rate of 2DPCA was superior to that of PCA, ICA, and Kernel Eigenfaces.

(4) Overall, an estimated 85 million adults aged 18–69 years in China were obese in 2018, which was three times as many as in 2004.

(5) The number of MUs and FUs is the same as that of traditional HetNets.

Unit 4 Results and Discussions

IV. Underline the words and phrases that are used to hedge or boost claims in the following paragraphs. Discuss with a partner why the authors choose to hedge or boost the claims.

The results presented previously clearly show that the accuracy of the geometric features of the steps is particularly affected by noise over larger distances. The problem was expected but to a lesser extent. More in general, the raw sensor data appears to be much noisier when acquired with Speedgoat compared to the initial tests done with the LIDAR directly connected to a PC. The authors' hypothesis is that the additional longer wiring and the conversion between serial protocols (UART to RS232) required by Speedgoat contribute to the noise. The issue could be mitigated by employing a LIDAR with better performance over long-range distances or by improving the signal-to-noise ratio of the current solution by improving the available hardware.

On the other hand, the most critical features of a step, namely the distance d from it and the step height h, are always estimated with significant precision. The slight deviation is easily compensated by the auxiliary checks done by the controller to verify if there is a contact or not between the wheels and the step. If desired, the LIDAR could be fixed higher on the chassis to obtain a better perspective to estimate the distance e; however, by doing so, the perspective could be not suited for estimating the step height h with the same quality.

Despite the problems, the step classification system proves to be robust during the entire experimental campaign. However, more research needs to be done on environmental factors that could affect sensor measures. In particular, this system has to be tested with steps made of different materials and with different lighting and weather conditions to evaluate how reflection, visibility, and light affect the measure. This open point is crucial to guarantee the same robustness achieved in a controlled laboratory environment, also in environmental conditions closer to real scenarios.

(Adapted from "Autonomous Detection and Ascent of a Step for an Electric Wheelchair" by A. Botta et al. in *Mechatronics*, 86, 2022.)

Project

Work in groups. Choose 3-4 journal articles from different authoritative international journals in your discipline and discuss the wording, style, and organization of the Results and Discussion sections. Prepare a presentation to be delivered in class.

Unit 5

Conclusions

Part I
Introducing the Unit

Most readers (including editors and reviewers) read the abstract and the conclusion of a journal article before they decide whether they would like to or need to go further and deeper. In the Conclusion section of an article, the authors summarize the findings and the importance of the study, discuss where ambiguity exists, and suggest further research. An effective conclusion should wind up an article and readers could make sense of the concepts and the ideas that are intended to be explained.

In this unit, we are going to focus on the structure and the main content of the typical conclusion of a journal article in the domains of science and technology.

After finishing this unit, you are expected to achieve the following learning objectives:

- to be acquainted with the structure and organization of the conclusion;
- to appropriately select the core content of the conclusion;
- to employ useful expressions to compose the conclusion that is acceptable by the academic community of the specific field.

Part II
Learning Useful Expressions

Study the bold-faced expressions that are often used in the conclusions of journal articles.

A. Summarizing the Topic

- Polls measuring the change in opinion **have been analyzed** using an abstraction of acceleration.
- **This study evaluated** the inhibitory activity of SnuCalCpIs against cathepsin L, which plays a crucial role in cancer cell migration through ECM degradation.
- **In this study**, the genetic variation in phenolic components and antioxidant activity of Iranian oregano accessions **was investigated**.
- **The present study generated** a cellobiose phosphorylase from the genome of C. bescii.
- **The current research draws attention towards the fact that** the use of different concentrations of the peptide powder can significantly affect the oxidative stability and functional properties of meat (beef) because of their well-known nutritional and health benefits.

B. Describing the Process

- The inhibition mechanism **was investigated by adopting a** bioinformatics **approach**.
- In this study, a weighed concentration of the dried milk casein protein hydrolysate (CPH) powder **was added to** the raw beef nuggets **in order to** check their established effects on the oxidative stability as well as the functional capability of the minced beef during refrigeration storage.
- **This research uses** IoT technology, wireless sensor technology, RFID technology, crawler technology, database technology, and other related technologies **to** design and implement a set of food traceability system **using** rice **as an example**.

C. Presenting the Findings

- The effects of media, including social media, **do not seem to** alter the acceleration of opinion as demonstrated over one hundred years of poll taking.

- We **characterize** several components in PAL, and **found that** pyruvate, acetate, and formate did not exhibit cytotoxicity against glioblastoma cells.
- FA profiles and healthy FA index in subcutaneous adipose tissue **differed** among three cattle breeds **in the current study**.
- A high variation **was observed** between the highest and lowest quantity of concentration of rosmarinic acid and other phenolics.
- **The analysis of** the enzymatic properties and kinetic mechanisms **revealed that** the half-life of the CbCBP was 6 h and 4 h at 65 ℃ and 75 ℃, indicating that good thermal stability.
- **The results acquired suggest that** these antioxidant rich or biologically active compounds can effectively retard and/or suppress the lipid-oxidation during the storage period.
- **Concisely, it can be concluded that** the addition of bioactive peptides (BAPs) in beef nuggets **have proven to be** efficacious in improving the quality of meat.

D. Describing the Limitations

- The study explores averages and the population **may experience more rapid changes in** opinion **over time**, but these are averaged out when considering the opposing opinions.
- **Although** the approach itself is generalizable, the models trained using this approach **are sufficiently discriminative of** the experimental conditions.
- Key genes such as SREBF1 may serve as the genetic markers for such selection, **but** validation of the potential marker genes in a larger population **is needed**.

E. Addressing the Values

- **This result not only supported the validity of** the MEM, **but also demonstrated the feasibility of** this method.
- Validation of three methods has been conducted and the mathematical model statistics **could explain the meaning of** the parameters.
- The newly defined physics-based GT **allows** deep learning **to** tackle the optically hard problem of out-of-focus light and PSF-associated blurring. **It also enables** correct identification of the structures that the models have been trained to recognize, even in the challenging cases of fluorescence bleed-through.
- This approach **is** also **generalizable across different types of** cell and

Unit 5 Conclusions

fluorophore. Transfer learning using smaller microscope-specific simulation-supervised datasets **is a suitable mechanism for** adopting the proposed paradigm across various fluorescence microscopy systems.

- **Accordingly, it may advance research in a variety of fields of** biology and biomedicine in which the results and fundamental knowledge are often derived from bioimage analysis.
- **The results strongly suggest that** our approach **is applicable to** a wide range of different automated analysis pipelines.
- We **highlight that the proposed method establishes** the utility of a physics-based simulation-supervised training approach for deep learning applications in the microscopy data of living cells. **This will open other research avenues in the future.**
- **More challenging and complicated structures of interest in** the life sciences, such as the endoplasmic reticulum and Golgi bodies, **can be simulated to** extend the applicability of this approach in life-science studies.
- **These findings represent a major step towards unraveling the great mystery of** how PAL causes the selective killing of cancer cells.
- **These results might be utilized for** breeding oregano plants containing a high quantity of phenolic components and exhibiting high antioxidant activity.
- **As a result**, identification of different accessions which are richest in special components **is very important for** food and pharmaceutical industries.
- **Finally, the survey of our study offers** a broad-ranging variability among the Iranian oregano populations for utilizing elite accessions and subspecies.
- **These conclusions**, in addition to the general approach outlined in this study, **may be useful for** reporting soil C accounts in a wider international context.
- **In summary**, the distinct properties of CbCBP **would facilitate its application in** the biodegradation of cellulose and the synthesis of functional oligosaccharides.
- Its addition in meat or meat-based products **can help in** curbing the deleterious quality effects along with storage of these products or the meat itself and hence **can promote** health which is the sole purpose of recent therapeutic food development researches.
- **The observations reported here can form the foundation for such research.**

F. Stating Future Research

- Additionally, **further research is needed to** verify MEM on different soil types and how to quantify Dc on gentle slopes especially with short length.
- **Further** morphological dynamics-based features **may be analyzed through** tracking and following the morphological changes of segmented structures, for example, as shown in Fig. 5.
- **We expect** the nexus between machine learning and biology **to only grow stronger, in the near future revolutionizing** both **our insights about** biological systems and the opportunities available to researchers in the life sciences.
- **However**, the elaborate mechanisms **need to be elucidated in further research**, in which the stereochemical study would be used as a means of determining the kinetic mechanisms of CbCBP.

Part III
Learning Ways of Organization

In this part, we are going to discuss the structures of conclusions so as to develop the skills of writing the conclusions of academic papers in science and technology.

The frequency of a Conclusion section included in a journal article is relatively lower than that of the Results section or the Discussion section or the Results and Discussion section. That is, not all journal articles comprise a Conclusion section. Generally speaking, a strong conclusion is an impressive one, because this is the last chance for writers to remind readers of the topic of the article. To achieve this, the major findings tend to be articulated at the very beginning rather than be implicitly expressed between the lines, with the whole main idea expressed in the opening statement and the following few sentences elaborating on it. The whole part should be brief, to the point, without new information or evidence (statistics, quotations, etc.), and in clear and concise language. The importance of the study should be highlighted to convince the readers and peers that the findings further or challenge the previous work in the field concerned. What is novel in the study should be highlighted, too, which is also what justifies the writing and publication of the article. Its content is not supposed to repeat the abstract but should answer the question(s) proposed in the introduction. Finally, the specific guidelines of certain journals should be catered to. Different journals may have different requirements of conclusions. Some require conclusions in the conventional sense, others combine conclusions with discussions, and still others require conclusions and perspectives.

Main Elements of a Complete Conclusion

A typical conclusion consists of three parts:

- Restating the main idea: Since every other section of the article supports the thesis, the conclusion should be the finale of the article. Yet restating is by no means repeating the main idea word by word. We should paraphrase the main idea and try to spark the readers' thinking and to persuade them in a subtle way to adopt our stand on the topic or willingly follow our recommendation. We should still refer back to our introduction.
- Summarizing (three) main points: It is unnecessary for us to restate every argument that we have made; we should only pick out three that we believe are the most impressive. We can then piece together the three arguments into one special force to further reinforce our main idea, giving credibility to our argument.
- Finishing on a high note or an epic closing line: It is better to end up the conclusion with an interesting and thought-provoking insight. This could be in the form of a rhetorical question, a striking quotation from the research, or some broader implications (not new information) or larger context.

Some Tips

Before writing the conclusion, we should ask ourselves these questions: "What should the readers remember from the article? How relevant are the results? Why should anyone be interested in this study? Is there any unanswered or new questions?" Thinking over and answering these questions may help us outline the structure of the conclusion and filter the content to decide what is in and what is out. When writing the conclusion, we should restate the hypothesis or research question and major findings and clarify the contributions that the study has made to the existing field. Any limitations of the study should be highlighted honestly and straightforward, and future directions for research or recommendations should be stated. Of course, we should always be proud of the case that we just made.

On the other hand, we should not include in the conclusion the information that should be included in the discussion, or vice versa, or introduce new arguments or new data. The use of the tiring "In conclusion…" is undesirable; our tone and thoughtful summarization should be injected into the article.

Differences Between Abstracts and Conclusions

Despite their similarities in summarizing the idea of the article, the abstract and the conclusion of an article are different in four important ways:

- Aim. The aim of the abstract is to allow readers to decide whether they would like to read further, while that of the conclusion is to remind readers of the selling points of the stated arguments and to push further research on a topic.
- Question answered. An abstract should answer the question "What?", while a conclusion answers the question "What next?".
- Citation of other scientific work. There should not be any citation in an abstract but there could be one or some in a conclusion.
- Summarization levels. An abstract summarizes an article at a very higher level than that of a conclusion.

To sum up, the conclusion should summarize all the concepts that we introduced in the main body of the article, in a sequence of the most important to the least important. We should not include any new concept in the conclusion.

Part IV
Analyzing the Examples

In this part, we are going to analyze some examples so as to understand the wording, structures, and moves of conclusions of academic papers in science and technology.

I. **Analyze the following Conclusion section and discuss the questions with a partner.**

Conclusion

In order to improve the degree of automation and intelligentization of straw

Unit 5 Conclusions

returning machine and solve the over and less tillage problem, navigation path detection algorithms of rice, rape, and wheat high crop stubble were studied. Findings are as follows:

1) Based on intensity mean value texture descriptor segmenting field images, it could effectively separate object area from soil background.

2) Shearing binary image before extracting navigation path candidate points was an effective method to dwindle the influence of the white spots in background area, and the navigation path candidate points could truly reflect the trend of navigation path, and be well robust. The use of the least square method for fitting navigation path has fast detection speed and high precision. Therefore, it could meet the need of real-time processing.

3) The experimental results proven that, navigation paths, derived by navigation path detection algorithm under different crop species (rice, rape, and wheat), all efficiently reflected the tillage boundary. The algorithm was adaptable.

(Adapted from "Automatic Navigation Path Detection Method for Tillage Machines Working on High Crop Stubble Fields Based on Machine Vision" by T. Zhang et al. in *International Journal of Agricultural and Biological Engineering*, 7(4), 2014.)

 Questions:

1. How is the conclusion organized?

2. What elements are included in the conclusion?

3. Is this a typical complete conclusion? Why or why not?

II. Compare the following three conclusions and answer the questions.

Conclusion 1

This study demonstrated an interactive effect between C/N ratio and temperature on the performance of anaerobic co-digestion of dairy manure, chicken manure, and rice straw. Our results suggest that increased temperature from mesophilic to thermophilic conditions resulted in ammonia inhibition; however, this kind of inhibition could be reduced or avoided by increasing the C/N ratio of mixed feedstock to an appropriate level. In anaerobic co-digestion of DM, CM, and RS, the optimal C/N level was 26.76 at 35 ℃ and 30.67 at 55 ℃. Adjusting the proportions of mixture substrates in anaerobic co-digestion to obtain suitable feed characteristics, such as the C/N ratio, pH, and nutrients, is an effective way to achieve desired digestion performance.

(Adapted from "Effects of Temperature and Carbon-nitrogen (C/N) Ratio on the Performance of Anaerobic Co-digestion of Dairy Manure, Chicken Manure and Rice Straw: Focusing on Ammonia Inhibition" by X. Wang et al. in *PLoS ONE*, 9(5), 2014.)

Conclusion 2

In this article, we have provided a comprehensive overview of radio RAAs in modern HetNets. We have introduced four cell types, such as macrocells, microcells, picocells, and femtocells, and five network scenarios of HetNets, i.e., traditional cellular HetNets, OFDMA-based HetNets, NOMA-based HetNets, relay-based HetNets, and multi-antenna HetNets. For each network scenario, the RAAs are presented according to approaches, criteria, techniques, purposes, and architectures. For each category, the available literature on RAAs is reviewed and summarized while analyzing the advantages and disadvantages of the adopted approaches. To help new starters conducting research in this field, we shed light on the related challenges and future research trends that need deep investigations. Moreover, to deal with the challenges of wireless big data and intelligent communications, we have proposed a learning-based RA structure and a control-based RA structure in HetNets. Since the RAAs in HetNets will play an important role in the next-generation wireless communication for providing seamless connection, high system capacity, massive connectivity, etc., it is anticipated that this survey will provide a quick and comprehensive understanding of the current state of the arts in RAAs for HetNets, which will attract more researchers into this area.

(Adapted from "A Survey on Resource Allocation for 5G Heterogeneous Networks: Current Research, Future Trends, and Challenges" by Y. Xu et al. in *IEEE Communications Surveys and Tutorials*, 23(2), 2021.)

Unit 5 Conclusions

Conclusion 3

The vibrationally state-selected ion-molecule reaction system of $N_2^+(X^2\Sigma_g^+; v^+ = 0\text{--}2) + C_2H_2$ has been studied by combining the high-resolution VUV-PFI-PI technique and the DQDO mass spectrometer developed in our laboratory. Detailed absolute integral cross sections and branching ratios for the CT and HT channels have been measured covering an unprecedentedly wide E_{cm} range of 0.03–10.00 eV. The integral cross section for the CT channel is found to decrease with the increase of the kinetic energy, but the opposite trend is observed of that for the HT channel. The E_{cm} dependence of the CT channel observed is consistent with a long-range exothermic CT mechanism, whereas that for the HT channel is partially enhanced by collision energies. The vibrationally selected cross-section measurements for both the CT and HT channels reveal only marginal vibrational effects. The comparison of the sum of $\sigma_{CT}(v^+) + \sigma_{HT}(v^+)$, for $v^+ = 0$, 1, and 2, shows that the reactivity of $N_2^+(v^+)$ towards C_2H_2 is slightly inhibited by vibrational excitation at low $E_{cm} < 0.60$ eV, whereas a slight enhancement is observed at high $E_{cm} > 1.00$ eV. Both the integral cross sections and the branch ratios obtained in the present work are valuable for benchmarking state-of-the-art theoretical calculations and for the modeling of the chemical composition of Titan's atmosphere.

(Adapted from "Absolute Integral Cross Sections for the State-selected Ion-molecule Reaction $N_2^+(X^2\Sigma_g^+; v^+ = 0\text{--}2) + C_2H_2$ in the Collision Energy Range of 0.03–10.00 eV" by Y. Xu et al. in *The Astrophysical Journal*, 827(1), 2016.)

 Questions:

1. What are the similarities between the three conclusions in terms of structure, content, and language use?

2. What are the differences between the three conclusions in terms of structure, content, and language use?

3. Are there any limitations of the research concerned mentioned in each of the three conclusions?

Exercises

I. Analyze the following Concluding Remarks section in terms of main elements of a typical conclusion.

Concluding Remarks

When multiple QoS-constrained applications share a processor resource such as LLC, it may be impossible to change the baseline LLC partitioning to improve energy efficiency without causing any performance degradation. Previous work proposed coordinated management of core resources such as VF or size of the microarchitectural components together with LLC partitioning to alleviate this problem. However, continuously tracking a fixed performance target can considerably limit the energy savings. Therefore, this article presents an alternative approach based on managing short-term performance slack.

It first demonstrates that slack can be generated at a relatively low energy cost and consumed later to save a larger amount of energy. Furthermore, it shows the possibility to transfer slack from one application to another, which enables more opportunities to improve energy savings. Based on these insights, an online resource management scheme, called Cooperative Slack Management (CSM), is presented to reduce processor energy while respecting the QoS of all applications. CSM is quantitatively evaluated against the previous approach and an extension with local slack management in several different scenarios. According to the evaluations, CSM can achieve substantial energy savings, even in scenarios when the other two schemes cannot save considerable energy. CSM is especially effective when the performance target is high, when the core architecture is fixed, and when there is high contention in LLC. For example, it can potentially save up to 41% energy in a case in which the savings with the other approaches is around 1%. With perfect models, the average potential energy savings range from 13% to 25% in different scenarios. However, when using the proposed modeling framework, this range reduces to 10% to 21% due to limited accuracy. That said, the proposed hybrid (active/passive) sampling technique provides a means to further improve modeling accuracy by selectively increasing the configurations that are actively sampled. This can be studied in future work.

(Adapted from "Cooperative Slack Management: Saving Energy of Multicore Processors by Trading Performance Slack Between QoS-Constrained Applications" by M. Nejat et al. in *ACM Transactions on Architecture and Code Optimization*, 19(2), 2022.)

II. Translate the following Chinese conclusion into English using the expressions listed below.

结论

本研究以生菜为例，利用修饰光敏色素信号途径对植物进行改良，经正交试验及验证试验分析，夜间增加远红光间断辐照下，种子萌发阶段无干旱胁迫，幼苗阶段设置轻度干旱胁迫为远红光促进生菜种子萌发及幼苗生长的最优方案，并且对散叶生菜促进效果最明显。本研究为设施农业生产中植物逆境胁迫提供一种新的环境友好型解决策略，可解决农业生产中的实际问题，对于光合农业具有极大的应用价值。

（选自"远红光辐照对干旱胁迫下生菜种子萌发及幼苗生长的影响"，栗昕羽等，《中国农业大学学报》，第 27 卷，第 5 期，2022 年）

Some expressions that might be used:

修饰光敏色素信号途径	modification of phytochrome signaling pathways
正交试验	the orthogonal test
验证试验	the verification experiment
增加远红光间断辐射	the intermittent supplementary irradiation of far-red light
干旱胁迫	drought stress
种子萌发	seed germination
幼苗生长	seedling growth
设施农业生产	the protected agriculture
植物逆境胁迫	the adversity stress that plants are faced with
光合农业	the photosynthetic agriculture

III. Below are the introduction and the conclusion of the same article. Analyze how the content of the conclusion refers back to that of the introduction.

Introduction

One of the central drivers of mathematical progress is the discovery of patterns and formulation of useful conjectures: statements that are suspected to be true but have not been proven to hold in all cases. Mathematicians have always used data to help in this process—from the early hand-calculated prime tables used by Gauss and others that led to the prime number theorem, to modern computer-generated data in cases such as the Birch and Swinnerton-Dyer conjecture. The introduction of computers to generate data and test conjectures afforded mathematicians a new understanding of problems that were previously inaccessible, but while computational techniques have become consistently useful in other parts of the mathematical process, artificial intelligence (AI) systems have not yet established a similar place. Prior systems for generating conjectures have either contributed genuinely useful research conjectures via methods that do not easily generalize to other mathematical areas, or have demonstrated novel, general methods for finding conjectures that have not yet yielded mathematically valuable results.

AI, in particular in the field of machine learning, offers a collection of techniques that can effectively detect patterns in data and has increasingly demonstrated utility in scientific disciplines. In mathematics, it has been shown that AI can be used as a valuable tool by finding counterexamples to existing conjectures, accelerating calculations, generating symbolic solutions, and detecting the existence of structure in mathematical objects. In this work, we demonstrate that AI can also be used to assist in the discovery of theorems and conjectures at the forefront of mathematical research. This extends work using supervised learning to find patterns by focusing on enabling mathematicians to understand the learned functions and derive useful mathematical insight. We propose a framework for augmenting the standard mathematician's toolkit with powerful pattern recognition and interpretation methods from machine learning and demonstrate its value and generality by showing how it led us to two fundamental new discoveries, one in topology and another in representation theory. Our contribution shows how mature machine learning methodologies can be adapted and integrated into existing mathematical workflows to achieve novel results.

Conclusion

In this work we have demonstrated a framework for mathematicians to use machine learning that has led to mathematical insight across two distinct disciplines: one of the first connections between the algebraic and geometric structure of knots and a proposed resolution to a long-standing open conjecture in representation theory. Rather than use machine learning to directly generate conjectures, we focus on helping guide the highly tuned intuition of expert mathematicians, yielding results that are both interesting and deep. It is clear that intuition plays an important role in elite performance in many human pursuits. For example, it is critical for top Go players and the success of AlphaGo came in part from its ability to use machine learning to learn elements of play that humans perform intuitively. It is similarly seen as critical for top mathematicians—Ramanujan was dubbed the Prince of Intuition and it has inspired reflections by famous mathematicians on its place in their field. As mathematics is a very different, more cooperative endeavor than Go, the role of AI in assisting intuition is far more natural. Here, we show that there is indeed fruitful space to assist mathematicians in this aspect of their work.

Our case studies demonstrate how a foundational connection in a well-studied and mathematically interesting area can go unnoticed, and how the framework allows mathematicians to better understand the behavior of objects that are too large for them to otherwise observe patterns in. There are limitations to where this framework will be useful—it requires the ability to generate large datasets of the representations of objects and for the patterns to be detectable in examples that are calculable. Further, in some domains the functions of interest may be difficult to learn in this paradigm. However, we believe there are many areas that could benefit from our methodology. More broadly, it is our hope that this framework is an effective mechanism to allow for the introduction of machine learning into mathematicians' work, and encourage further collaboration between the two fields.

(Adapted from "Advancing Mathematics by Guiding Human Intuition with AI" by A. Davies et al. in *Nature, 600*(7887), 2021.)

IV. Read the following two conclusions. The first one is taken from an article in geography (natural sciences) and the second one from an article in anthropology (social sciences). Compare them in terms of language use, structure, and style.

Conclusion 1

The pandemic, due to SARS-CoV-2, a novel coronavirus, has a far-reaching effect on every person around the world. It showed a drastic effect on every sector of the economy. Lockdown caused due to COVID-19 impacted the economic circulation around the world, which resulted in shut down of production units, business at national and international level. In this study, the possible significant impacts of phase-wise lockdown due to COVID-19 on No_2 concentration in eight districts of India using Sentinel-5P satellite images of the European Space Agency and CPCB ground-based monitoring station data were analyzed and compared with the same periods in 2019. The results demonstrated a drastic reduction in the levels of No_2 concentration in these regions. It was observed that the data obtained from the satellite-based monitoring system differed from ground station data for few study regions. If sector-specific (power plants, industries, transportation, construction) emission and production data become available during the lockdown period, then many cost-specific air pollution policies could be formulated. Future research on these issues is warranted to understand the full implications and draw valuable policy lessons from this unprecedented event.

(Adapted from "Phase-wise Spatial and Temporal Variations of Nitrogen Dioxide During and pre COVID-19 Lockdown Period in Tier-1 Cities of India" by K. Ashwini et al. in *Spatial Information Research*, 29(6), 2021.)

Conclusion 2

In the last decade, roughly, two major population turnovers were identified by ancient DNA studies: the "Early Neolithic" (6600 BC – 5000 BC) and the "Late Neolithic" or "Early Bronze Age" (3000 BC – 2000 BC). This had an enormous effect on our view of prehistory and, especially, our views on the importance of human mobility in social change. However, the narratives connected to these turnovers show a stark imbalance between the sophistication of biological work and archaeological contextualization. Initially overwhelmed by the analytical and computational power of aDNA studies, by the impact of the natural scientific publication system, archaeologists failed to contribute to an interdisciplinary discourse with the theoretical sophistication and empirical base of knowledge available. Instead, the aDNA data were included in overgeneralizing, simplistic narratives, heavily biased by long-outdated 20th century culture-historical views of collectively migrating, biologically homogeneous social groups with too little regard for anthropological or archaeological theory or the current knowledge of the archaeological record. The main flaw of the narratives spun around both periods—the Early Neolithic and the Early Bronze Age—is the idea of monothetic archaeological cultures or, at a deeper level, the mindset behind such a kind of concept, the idea of the existence of clearly bounded, internally homogeneous groups of people, the essentializing of ethnic identities. Add to this a good portion of Western stereotypes about gender roles and the nature of human agency, and the results are the kind of narratives put forward about the newly discovered migrations in prehistory.

If we pick apart those biases and prejudices, the scenarios for human movement during the Early Neolithic and the Early Bronze Age will be more complicated and regionally diverse. The alternative narratives proposed here are less concrete and less easy to communicate because they allow for and acknowledge regionally and locally specific histories, modifications of overall influences, and trends that are clearly indicated by the diversity of the archaeological record. It is still possible, however, to reasonably discuss main drivers or even prime movers of these trans-continental clusters of connected movements, in both timeframes deriving from southwest Asia, where two of the most consequential transformations of social and economic systems during human history took place. The first brought agriculture, animal husbandry, and sedentary village life; the second is connected to a new ideological system that to a higher degree than before featured violent coercion, more fixed and unequal gender relations, and individual aggrandizement that took hold in European communities, changes that later became more important in Bronze Age and Iron Age societies.

(Adapted from "Mobility and Social Change: Understanding the European Neolithic Period After the Archaeogenetic Revolution" by M. Furholt in *Journal of Archaeological Research, 29*, 2021.)

Project

Work in groups. Choose 3–4 journal articles from different authoritative international journals and discuss the wording, style, and organization of the conclusions. Prepare a presentation to be delivered in class.

Unit 6

Review Articles

Part I
Introducing the Unit

In scientific journals, comments on the development in the past or the review of the recent progress are always demonstrated in the form of review articles, while in long papers like dissertation or thesis, literature reviews would undertake the tasks of reviewing the current progress and concluding the past development. A review article is not simply a list of papers already published on a specific topic or a short summary of the important topics. It should include a theme, a research body, and a point of view. It should contain one or more of the following elements: description of different approaches towards the measurement, design, fabrication, or modeling of a specific item; a specific tool, process, or method for different applications; a new idea gained from the topic or new problem issue previously unnoticed; two or more competing theories or explanations of a phenomenon, with evidence for each; process of theory in different disciplines; comparison of the major discovery or concept and their advantages or disadvantages. Review articles convey the newest messages and help improve the quality of future research. Writing a review article involves reading relevant texts and other related articles in detail and finally presenting a well-informed judgment of the topic. Review articles put forward opinions by providing an alternative viewpoint on previously unknown relations among distinct studies.

In this unit, we are going to learn about the structure, content, and language use of review articles and how to summarize and evaluate the research on a given topic in a proper way.

After finishing this unit, you are expected to achieve the following learning objectives:

- to analyze the results to make a summary or synthesize the contents;
- to assess the strengths, patterns, and trends in the literature;
- to identify the weakness, contradictions, and research gaps in the literature, and recommend new areas;
- to draw a conclusion based on the data from various resources.

Unit 6　Review Articles

Part II
Learning Useful Expressions

Study the bold-faced expressions that are often used in the literature reviews of journal articles.

A. Stating the Summary

- Successful therapy method **in combination with** radiation therapy and/or chemotherapy is provided to the cancer patient which **proven to be beneficial to** the patients.
- **Research has shown that** elevated body temperature can damage and kill cancerous cells with minimal injury to normal cells.
- Given the obesity epidemic that has recently emerged in developed societies, **the specific study of factors** that determine food ingestion in humans has become particularly urgent.
- **It is widely appreciated that** plaque rupture is an important component of ACS.
- **These findings reveal** essential genomic **information** considering the newly identified hyper-aerotolerant Campylobacter lari strain SCHSO$_2$.
- Climate change is suspected **though not proven to** have been a factor in a string of diseases outbreaks.
- **The major distinctions** between 4D and 3D printing are smart design and smart materials, as 4D printed structures may change shape or function.
- Sensory aspects, such as the appearance and taste of these products, **are crucial factors** for the consumer quality evaluation and their consumption on a regular basis.
- **The study also provided some interesting findings** pertaining to the perception of specific ingredients.
- **Another noteworthy finding** was that the first MFA dimension indicated a perceived trade-off between taste and health.
- The European Union (EU) **has acknowledged these negative effects** of our food production system, and to limit climate change, the EU advocates a more sustainable food production system.
- **With respect to the differences** in the PM results, visual inspection of the

HMFA analysis shows the partial points are close to the consensus point.

- **Taken collectively**, the results show that length of the recipe was the most important factor consumers considered.
- **From the cumulative score of** healthy food interest, we **found no significant difference** between dietary groups.

B. Describing the Procedures

- We also **summarize the current applications of** m^{6}A writers and erasers for m^{6}A detection and **highlight the merits and drawbacks** of these available methods.
- The existence of m^{6}A **was first reported** in mRNA from mammalian cells in the 1970s.
- **Another contributory factor** is that the CT contains clusters of cells within that group.
- **Since then**, m^{6}A-related proteins have been vastly studied and successively identified.
- There are over 100 types of cancers present in the world and **are classified according to** cell type.
- Various techniques of hyperthermia **are presently under investigation**, that include local, regional, and whole-body hyperthermia.
- Attaining temperature above the systemic temperature 37 ℃ in a specified target volume is a challenge and still **under development**.

C. Illustrating the Significance of the Research

- Whole-body hyperthermia **is applied to** treat metastatic tumor that has spread throughout the body.
- The power distribution **is influenced by** three-dimensional anatomy.
- Hence, radiotherapy and hyperthermia **are complementary** in their action.
- Data reported in 2004 revealed that the thermal inhibition of the non-homologous end-joining pathway **plays a role in** thermal radio sensitization.
- However, few data suggested that the homologous recombination pathway **may not be the major heat target**.

D. Justifying the Research

- **Another theoretical finding** was that the endmost oscillator in the normal hand model stabilized to a lower frequency mode as time elapsed.

- **The onus remains on** researchers to design and evaluate multilevel interventions that further stimulate policy thinking while providing the robust level of evidence needed to drive change.
- **This is why** we should study human food intake behavior.
- A clinical study of hyperthermia along with radiotherapy **was associated** from 1989 to 1998.
- Multicentric investigation showed that **combination therapy** of hyperthermia **with** radiotherapy improves the results when compared with the radiotherapy or hyperthermia alone.
- But till now **either ad hoc cost functional** based on the thermal distribution or on the absorption rate density has been used for regional hyperthermia.
- **This planning greatly improves** the quality of medical treatment with a virtual experiment to model, and **optimizes** the therapy with high accuracy.

Part III
Learning Ways of Organization

In this part, we are going to discuss the structures of review articles so as to develop the skills of writing review articles of academic papers in science and technology.

Types of Review Articles

Review articles can be classified into three main categories according to their methods or approaches: narrative, systematic, and meta-analysis articles.

Narrative Review Articles

Narrative reviews adopt the traditional approach, and generally do not include the method description. These articles are selected on the basis of experience and subjectivity of the experts in this area who may employ different methodologies and then draw a conclusion. It provides an overview of these articles and analyzes the results on a qualitative level.

Systematic Review Articles

The authors of the systematic review articles have systematically searched, appraised, and summarized the studies in the specific area. The data would be collected by using a clearly-defined and reproducible methodology. Unlike narrative reviews, systematic reviews aim to minimize bias by using explicit criteria to obtain objective information as they often select evidence-based science articles.

Meta-analysis Review Articles

The meta-analysis review articles compare and combine the findings of previously published studies, usually to assess the effectiveness of a method. As they are focused on the method, the language tends to be objective and the list of methods will be collected according to the time sequence. Every method would be described in great detail.

Review articles can be invited or unsolicited submissions. Invited review articles are written by the experts in the relevant field of study. Unsolicited submissions are written after researchers have chosen to study a particular field of interest.

General Structure of Review Articles

Review articles are typically twice as long as most regular journal articles, with hundreds of references. Mini-reviews tend to focus on a recent "hot topic" that has only a limited amount of accumulated literature. They tend to be about half the length and number of citations as full reviews due to their narrower scope. Still, they can be very valuable to readers if they accomplish the goals of organization and synthesis. This helps to define the scope of the review, which then drives the literature search to move towards this direction. The unique contribution that the authors of a review paper can make is the organization and synthesis of the knowledge found in the literature. Thus, deciding upon this organization and executing on the synthesis of the past work are where the authors truly add value with their review. The general structure of review articles should include the following four parts.

Part 1 Description

Step 1: Summary—Describing the Hypothesis or Major Objectives of the Research

e.g., Bone tissues are one of the most complex tissues in the body that regenerate and repair themselves spontaneously under the right physiological conditions. Within the limitations of treating bone defects, mimicking tissue engineering through the recruitment of scaffolds, cell sources, and growth factors, is strongly recommended.

Step 2: Summary—Describing the Development

e.g., Over the past decades, cancer is the major cause of incidence of death increasing every day. Different forms of tumor therapy including radiotherapy and chemotherapy are used to treat cancer. However, hyperthermia is the technique that neglects the use of chemicals or harmful radiations.

Step 3: Outlining the Theme

e.g., The objective of this article is to review the role HMGB1 in brain injury and its immunomodulatory properties.

Part 2 Introduction

Step 1: Generalizing the Past Research

e.g., For the planned primary analysis of failure-free survival, we calculated that approximately 79 disease recurrence events or deaths in 362 patients would provide 80% power to detect a target hazard ratio (HR) of 0.52 with a log-rank test at a two-sided α level of 5%. After allowing for 10% dropout, we estimated that a total of 402 patients were needed (201 patients in each group). The intention-to-treat population (all randomized patients) was used for the analysis of efficacy. We also analyzed failure-free survival in the per-protocol population, which included all patients who did not violate the eligibility criteria and who had started the randomly assigned treatment (i.e., received at least one dose of capecitabine) or observation. Safety data were summarized for all patients (regardless of whether they had a violation of the eligibility criteria) who had started the randomly assigned treatment or observation (safety population).

Step 2: Defining the Terms

e.g., This protein is an intranuclear non-histone protein with a molecular weight of 30-kDa and is a mediator of inflammation and inflammatory responses following tissue damage (injury or infection) hence it is considered an important late inflammatory mediator. Several studies revealed that HMGB1 has molecular impact in pathogen-associated molecular patterns (PAMPs) in infection and damage-associated molecular patterns (DAMPs) in injury. Previous studies showed that

HMGB1 has involved in molecular mechanisms of systemic lidocaine treatment for closed fracture musculoskeletal injury in animal model.

Step 3: Stating the Main Findings

e.g., There are three cell types that are responsible for homeostasis in bone tissues and they are listed in the following: osteoblasts, which are derived from mesenchymal stem cells, make bone formation through the simulation of transcription factor RUNX-2 (runt-related factor 2) and osterix expression. Osteocytes are the mature osteoblasts that have the ability to build osteon in the bone matrix and affect the function of other bone cells. Osteoclasts, derived from hematopoietic stem cells, have bone resorption activity and express specific markers such as tartrate resistant acid phosphatase (TRAP), calcitonin receptor (CTR), and cathepsin-K (CTSK). The functional mechanism of different intercellular signaling molecules is the interactions between osteoblasts and osteocytes. Bone metabolism is affected by many endogenous and exogenous factors (Hadjidakis & Androulakis, 2006).

Step 4: Evaluating the Research

e.g., In this review, the new data related to aspirin are gathered and the impact of its parameters are discussed in the following. Its mechanism and chemical reactions in the physiological conditions are considered in the present article for first time. Moreover, its antimicrobial properties and ASP dose-mechanism relationships were discussed (Fig. 1).

Part 3 Body

Step 1: Illustrating the Research in Detail

e.g., One study, a new class of degradable shape-memory polymers (SMP) and thermoplastic copolymerized D, L-lactide, and 5%–10% aspirin-activated monomers (AspGA) was prepared. Effective aspirin interactions modulated the thermal and mechanical properties, which resulted a significant increase in toughness and thermal healing properties. The memory-shape refers to the property of an alloy that deforms upon cooling and returns to its original state with heat that this feature in this scaffold is in the physiological temperature range. The hydrolytic decomposition of this scaffold not only had no negative or reducing effect on bone formation, but the release of aspirin reduced acute inflammation (Xu et al., 2021). A series of 3D aspirin-loaded polylactic acid/graphene oxide (PLA/GO) porous biomimetic nanofibrous composite scaffolds (PBNCSs) were prepared by phase separation. GO nanoparticles significantly improved their hydrophilic properties and reduced their mechanical properties, but stabilized them thermally. Addition of GO nanoparticles improved the precipitation of hydroxyapatite on the scaffold. In general, this scaffold showed high biocompatibility and stable release performance. Aspirin loading within this scaffold, not only reduces inflammation, but also accelerates bone repair. The structure of this nanofiber scaffold provides a good space for aspirin to be released. In addition, the addition of GO nanoparticles, along with aspirin in the scaffold, stimulates the formation of bone-like apatite (Liu et al., 2020b).

Step 2: Explaining the Components

e.g., Ten different HMGB1 receptors have been described. They were TLR/MD-2, RAGE, CD24, Integrin, TIM3, TLR4, TLR2, TLR3, IL-1R1, and CXCR4. The effects of binding of HMGB1 with the respective receptors are described.

Step 3: Synthesizing the Goal

e.g., Granulomatous diseases of the nose and sinuses represent an uncommon but clinically important and potentially lethal group of disorders encountered in otolaryngology practice. A high index of suspicion, coupled with timely diagnosis and appropriate medical and surgical management, is required in the patient population. This paper will introduce the current diagnostic and classification scheme of infectious, inflammatory, and neoplastic granulomatous conditions affecting the sinonasal tract. Pertinent endoscopic, radiologic, and histologic findings will be highlighted in order to exemplify the typical clinical picture of these granulomatous diseases. Contemporary management strategies, including topical sinonasal and systemic therapies and the role of sinonasal surgery, will be reviewed.

Part 4 Results

Step 1: Drawing a Conclusion

e.g., Hyperthermia is today an important treatment modality in the treatment of cancer, and its results are strongly supported by the criteria of evidence-based medicine. Hyperthermia, in addition to radiotherapy with or without chemotherapy, is important when it is necessary to treat advanced or high-risk tumors, or to retreat a relapse in a pre-irradiated area. Hyperthermia appears to be the fourth pillar besides surgery, radiotherapy, and chemotherapy. Its diffusion is to be hoped for because, against the common enemy, four weapons are better than three.

Step 2: Making a Prospect

e.g., Despite recent significant progress in 2D material-based composite PCMs for thermal energy storage, heat transfer, energy conversion, and advanced multifunction, there are still several issues to be solved, mainly including the following key points:

(1) Although versatile 2D materials have widespread applications in many fields, the types of 2D materials currently used in thermal storage field are relatively limited. In the future, new-type 2D materials and their derivatives are urgently developed for PCMs, such as layered double hydroxides (LDHs), 2D metal-organic frameworks (MOFs) and covalent-organic frameworks (COFs), graphitic carbon nitride ($g\text{-}C_3N_4$), transition metal sulfides (TMDs), graphyne, metal nanosheets.

(2) Single layer MXene nanosheets are easily oxidized to titanium oxide, which may affect the chemical stability of MXene, especially in electric/solar-thermal applications at high temperatures. Therefore, great attention should be paid to the thermal robustness of 2D MXene.

(3) Although 2D MXene, phosphorene, MoS_2, and $g\text{-}C_3N_4$ have been applied to stabilize PCMs, they are still in infancy, and it deserves further researches to improve their thermophysical performances of composite PCMs.

By reading the following review article taken from *Future Foods Surgery*, we can see how a different structure is applied.

Abstract

Substitution of beef with alternative proteins is one practical trend taken by industry and consumers to reduce the negative impact of convenience products on the environment. Numerous products based on plant, insect, and fungi proteins compete to replace beef burgers in an environmentally friendly and healthy way. At the same time, there is a lack of studies which assess different options from an environmental impact perspective but also with consideration of production scales, recipes, nutritional values, and sensory properties. Therefore, the current study aimed to perform a holistic assessment (Life Cycle Assessment, sensory properties, and nutritional profile) of beef burgers in comparison to selected, alternative burgers, available on the market in Germany. The results indicated that alternative burgers based on plant, insect, and mycoprotein biomass would be more environmentally friendly than beef burgers, but only a couple of them (insect-based and soy-based) have satisfying sensory or nutritional properties. Pea-based and mycoprotein-based burgers were perceived as average burgers from an environmental and sensorial perspective. The study demonstrated a sustainability differentiation system of meat analogs in convenience products using the multicriteria framework with inclusion of nutrient scoring, sensorial testing, and Life Cycle Assessment.

1. Introduction

2. Methods

    2.1   Nutritional score

    2.2   Sensory testing

        2.2.1   Data collection

        2.2.2   Methods

        2.2.3   Regression Model

    2.3   LCA-goal and scope definition

        2.3.1   Objectives

        2.3.2   Functional unit

        2.3.3   System boundaries

        2.3.4   Data acquisition

        2.3.5   Limitations and assumptions

    2.4   Life cycle inventory

    2.5   Life Cycle Impact Assessment (LCIA)

3. Theory

4. Results

    4.1   Nutritional score

    4.2   Sensory testing and consumer acceptance results

        4.2.1   Hedonic scale

        4.2.2   Just-About-Right (JAR)

        4.2.3   Willingness-to-buy and willingness-to-pay

        4.2.4   Linear regression analysis

    4.3   Interpretation of LCA results

5. Discussion

6. Conclusions

    Declaration of Competing Interests

    Acknowledgments

(Adapted from "Meat Substitution in Burgers: Nutritional Scoring, Sensorial Testing, and Life Cycle Assessment" by S. Smetana et al. in *Future Foods*, *4*, 2021.)

    Similar to the research, the review article begins with an abstract. The introduction of a review article in a journal is typically one paragraph long and two or three paragraphs long for a longer book review. It should be less than 1/5 the length of the paper. The introduction in the review article should provide necessary background information that will be helpful to understand the forthcoming discussion. Then the authors will try to point out the aim of the paper and summarize the main findings or key arguments, and outline the order in which the readers will discuss it. The introduction will end with an evaluation of the review article. It can be a positive or negative evaluation or, as is usually the case, a mixed response.

    In the review article, the analysis part is the main body of the paper. Sometimes the body consists of findings and critiques. The authors will explain the methods adopted and demonstrate them with tables, charts, or pictures. The theory based or the results formed or the evaluation made will follow the Methods part. The authors give evidence to substantiate the interpretation of the data. A critical response should be balanced and well considered including both positive and negative statements. It is important to include other referenced sources to support the evaluation, and to link and compare between studies. The critique should be based on certain criteria, such as the following:

- What is the main point or argument in the article?
- Do the points of other authors concur with or differ from the arguments in the article?
- Do the authors' ideas help or hinder their arguments?
- Are the methods used sufficient to meet the study's aims, or reported in such a manner that the study's conclusions can be relied upon? (e.g., is it a double-blinded and randomized clinical trial?)
- Does the paper possess any bias?
- Are the authors qualified to make such claims?

The conclusion part leaves a lasting impression on the readers, and gains their interest for further developments in that field. The conclusion is typically a very short paragraph, in which the authors firmly state their overall stand for the thesis. They are required to succinctly summarize all the main points covered, point out the significance of these results, and ensure that they have clear take-home messages that integrate the points discussed in the review.

Part IV
Analyzing the Examples

In this part, we are going to analyze some examples so as to understand the wording, structures, and moves of review articles of academic papers in science and technology.

I. **Analyze the following summary of a review article and discuss the questions with a partner.**

Background

In China, mean body-mass index (BMI) and obesity in adults have increased steadily since the early 1980s. However, to our knowledge, there has been no reliable assessment of recent trends, nationally, regionally, or in certain population subgroups. To address this evidence gap, we present detailed analyses of relevant data from six consecutive nationally representative health surveys done between 2004 and 2018. We aimed to examine the long-term and recent trends in mean BMI and prevalence of obesity among Chinese adults, with specific emphasis on changes before and after 2010 (when various national non-communicable disease prevention programs were initiated), assess how these trends might vary by sex, age, urban-rural locality, and socioeconomic status, and estimate the number of people who were obese in 2018 compared with 2004.

Methods

We used data from the China Chronic Disease and Risk Factors Surveillance program, which was established in 2004 with the aim to provide periodic nationwide data on the prevalence of major chronic diseases and the associated behavioral and metabolic risk factors in the general population. Between 2004 and 2018, six nationally representative surveys were done. 776,571 individuals were invited and 746,020 (96.1%) participated, including 33,051 in 2004, 51,050 in 2007, 98,174 in 2010, 189,115 in 2013, 189,754 in 2015, and 184,876 in 2018. After exclusions, 645,223 participants aged 18–69 years remained for the present analyses. The mean BMI and prevalence of obesity (BMI ⩾ 30 kg/m^2) were calculated and time trends compared by sex, age, urban-rural locality, geographical region, and socioeconomic status.

Findings

Standardized mean BMI levels rose from 22.7 kg/m^2 (95% CI 22.5–22.9) in 2004 to 24.4 kg/m^2 (24.3–24.6) in 2018 and obesity prevalence from 3.1% (2.5–3.7) to 8.1% (7.6–8.7). Between 2010 and 2018, mean BMI rose by 0.09 kg/m^2 annually (0.06–0.11), which was half of that reported during 2004–2010 (0.17 kg/m^2, 95% CI 0.12–0.22). Similarly, the annual increase in obesity prevalence was somewhat smaller after 2010 than before 2010 (6.0% annual relative increase, 95% CI 4.4–7.6 vs 8.7% annual relative increase, 4.9–12.8; $p = 0.13$). Since 2010, the rise in mean BMI and obesity prevalence has slowed down substantially in urban men and women, and moderately in rural men, but continued steadily in rural women. By 2018, mean BMI was higher in rural than urban women (24.3 kg/m^2 vs 23.9 kg/m^2; $p = 0.0045$), but remained lower in rural than urban men (24.5 kg/m^2 vs 25.1 kg/m^2;

$p = 0.0007$). Across all six surveys, mean BMI was persistently lower in women with higher levels of education compared with women with lower levels of education, but the inverse was true among men. Overall, an estimated 85 million adults (95% CI 70 million–100 million; 48 million men [95% CI 39 million–57 million] and 37 million women [31 million–43 million]) aged 18–69 years in China were obese in 2018, which was three times as many as in 2004.

Interpretation

In China, the rise in mean BMI among the adult population appears to have slowed down over the past decade. However, we found divergent trends by sex, geographical area, and socioeconomic status, highlighting the need for a more targeted approach to prevent further increases in obesity in the Chinese general population.

Funding

China National Key Research and Development Program, China National Key Project of Public Health Program, and Youth Scientific Research Foundation of the National Center for Chronic and Non-communicable Disease Control and Prevention, Chinese Center for Disease Control and Prevention.

(Adapted from "Body-mass Index and Obesity in Urban and Rural China: Findings from Consecutive Nationally Representative Surveys During 2004–2018" by L. Wang et al. in *The Lancet, 398*(10294), 2021.)

 Questions:

1. What is the function of the summary in the review article?

2. Why is background information introduced in this summary?

3. Can the Interpretation part be omitted? Give your reasons.

II. Analyze the following excerpt and discuss the questions with a partner.

Vitamin D and Its Role in Parkinson's Disease Patients with SARS-CoV-2 Infection

Abstract

A novel coronavirus reportedly called 2019-nCoV started to spread around the world at the end of 2019. Severe acute respiratory syndrome coronavirus 2 (SARS-

CoV-2) was later renamed after links with SARS were observed. Multiple studies have reported possible connections between the COVID-19 virus and neurodegenerative diseases, including Parkinson's disease. Theories support that vitamin D deficiency plays a part in the pathogenicity of Parkinson's disease or the credibility of the associated dopamine system. Administration of vitamin D_3 was shown to significantly enhance the motor and non-motor manifestations of Parkinson's disease and enhance the quality of life. Also, multiple recent reviews have shown specific ways in which vitamin D reduces the risk of pathogenic infections. Recent studies supported the potential role of vitamin D in reducing the risk of COVID-19 infections and mortality. On the immunological level, immune response regulation remains one of the well-recognized actions of vitamin D. Vitamin D deficiency has been linked to complications in patients with SARS-CoV-2 infection and Parkinson's disease. Whereas more studies are required, vitamin D supplementation with a moderate and well-calculated dosage of vitamin D_3 in patients with Parkinson's disease can help minimize the risk and burden of COVID-19 complications.

1. Introduction

1.1 COVID-19: An Overview

A novel coronavirus reportedly called 2019-nCoV started to spread around the world at the end of 2019. Severe acute respiratory syndrome coronavirus 2 (SARS-CoV-2) was later renamed after certain SARS links were observed. The subsequent SARS-CoV-2 disease was referred to as coronavirus disease in 2019 (COVID-19). SARS-CoV-2, like SARS and Middle East Respiratory Syndrome (MERS), is a beta coronavirus primarily engaged in bats. Like most of the other coronaviruses, SARS-CoV-2 is a non-segmented, positive, single-stranded RNA virus. SARS-CoV-2 binds to the angiotensin-converting enzyme 2 (ACE2) receptor on pneumocytes Type I and Type II. Several manifestations of COVID-19 include fever, cough, and dyspnea, with pneumonia development in addition to sepsis in more severe cases. The more severe cases will lead to conspicuous hypoxemia and a need for respiratory support therapies. This pro-inflammatory condition can contribute to acute respiratory distress syndrome and cytokine storm syndrome (CSS), possibly induced by a maladaptive immune reaction involving interleukin-6 (IL-6), tumor necrosis factor-alpha (TNF-Ⅲ), interferon-gamma (IFN-y), interleukin-1 beta (IL-1β), and other provocative signaling pathways. Potential immune-impacting options have been introduced to provide preventive benefits or to reduce the incidence of COVID-19. Vitamin D is one of these options.

1.2 Vitamin D: An Overview

Vitamin D level and its concerning regulation with the parathyroid hormone activity (PTH) and the maintenance of the calcium and phosphate levels are to be balanced in according to needs. Vitamin D is acquired into the body either by exposure to sunlight and by food or supplementation. Vitamin D precursor (7-dehydrocholesterol) is synthesized in the human skin by ultraviolet (UVB) rays, where it becomes vitamin D_3. Vitamins D_2 and D_3 can be acquired directly from supplementation and fatty fish and milk products. Vitamin D are supported by cereals, beverages, and some non-dairy products. Vitamin D deficiency leads to any complications including neurological disorders. On the immunological level, immune response regulation remains one of the well-recognized actions of vitamin D antigen-presenting cells that could effectively metabolize the precursor of 25-hydroxyvitamin D (25D) to active 1,25-dihydroxyvitamin D. And that supports the interplay of vitamin D with immunity. Findings that immune activated cells expressed sub-cellular vitamin D receptors indicated a possible vitamin D role as an endogenous spatial modulation or immune responses. At the current pandemic of COVID-19, some randomized clinical trials and meta-analyses claim that vitamin D supplementation has benefits protecting against the development of COVID-19 manifestations. Some retrospective case-control studies have shown a link between vitamin D and COVID-19 incidents and complications, whereas other studies did not show any association when confounding factors were modified.

1.3 Vitamin D and Parkinson's Disease: An Overview

Studies on the relationship of vitamin D deficiency with Parkinson's disease (PD) have shown contradictory results. An observational prospective cohort study found that there was inadequate evidence to support the theory that vitamin D deficiency played a part in the pathogenicity of Parkinson's disease or the credibility of the associated dopamine system. However, other studies, including a randomized control trial and a comparative study, have indicated a higher prevalence of vitamin D deficiency in Parkinson's disease patients, clarifying the inverse association between serum levels 25-hydroxyvitamin D and the incidence of Parkinson's disease. Vitamin D supplementation was shown to decrease the rate of loss of motor activity as defined by both the Hoehn and Yahr scale and the Unified Parkinson's Disease Rating Scale (UPDRS) in an RCT. In another study, it was found that increased vitamin D levels could minimize the risk of Parkinson's disease. It is still too early to know if COVID-19 will have long-term effects on patients with PD and movement disorders patients. The global exposure of the frail and those with comorbid conditions, along with the increased incidence of PD with age, raises questions about the possible increased risk of COVID-19 in persons with PD and other movement disorders.

In contrast, the capacity to deliver routine neurological treatment is undermined by the burden on medical services exacerbated by this outbreak. In a current manner, presently there is inadequate evidence to suggest that PD alone raises the risk of COVID-19. Hypothetically, vitamin D may affect the outcome for COVID-19 patients with PD due to its role in regulating the response.

(Adapted from "Vitamin D and Its Role in Parkinson's Disease Patients with SARS-CoV-2 Infection" by A. Y. Azzam et al. in *Interdisciplinary Neurosurgery*, *27*, 2022.)

 Questions:

1. What are the characteristics of the title in this review article?

2. What are the characteristics of the abstract in this review article?

3. What is the function of the three overviews in the introduction?

Exercises

I. Read the following mini review article and identify the topic of the review article. Then decide what kind of review article it is. A narrative review article, a systematic review article, or a meta-analysis review article?

Carbon Neutrality Needs a Circular Metal-energy Nexus

Abstract

Carbon neutrality requires systematic transformations of both energy and metal systems. These transformations are not isolated but rather interlinked and interdependent, such that trade-offs between different strategies exist. Herein, we explore the critical interlinkages between energy and metal systems and further propose a circular metal-energy nexus to advance global coordinated actions towards a carbon-neutral future.

Keywords

carbon neutrality; metal-energy nexus; circular economy; critical metals; industrial ecology; green system engineering

1. Introduction

Carbon neutrality is gaining international political traction to avert the pressing climate crisis, which will evoke a systematic transformation in all industrial and service sectors. Among these, energy and materials are critical provisioning systems that are pivotal to the key functions of modern society. Previous studies have highlighted the urgent need for low-carbon transition in the energy system (i.e., renewable energy expansion, electrification, negative emission technologies, energy efficiency, etc.), or have only focused on the material system (i.e., material efficiency, eco-design, recycling, production technologies breakthroughs, etc.). Some of these proposed actions may reinforce, redistribute, or create new burdens that may intensify climate mitigation difficulties. Nexus thinking has been proposed as a key approach to addressing these systematic challenges.

In the context of carbon neutrality, systems of material production and energy supply are becoming increasingly interlinked and interdependent, particularly metallic materials (metals) and renewable energy technologies. Nevertheless, a nexus view of energy and materials remains an important, yet unexplored research area. At present, material production (mainly steel and other metals as hard-to-abated energy consumers) is an emergent large greenhouse gas (GHG) emitter and the low-carbon energy transition is critical to "limiting global warming to 1.5 ℃ by 2050". Based on various real-world examples and preliminary assessments, this perspective aims to offer a deeper understanding of the critical interlinkages of energy and material (mainly metals) systems to alert emerging challenges and to inform effective carbon-neutral strategies.

2. Energy Supply Dependence on Metals

Photovoltaics, wind turbines, electric vehicles, fuel cells, and other key infrastructures must be deployed on a large scale to achieve a carbon-neutral target. However, these infrastructures are much more material-intensive. For instance, photovoltaic power requires up to 40 times more copper than fossil fuel combustion power, and onshore wind power requires 8-fold that of the mineral requirement of a gas-fired plant of the same capacity. Notably, these low-carbon infrastructures also require large quantities of over 30 types of specialty raw materials (mainly metals), such as rare earths, cobalt, and lithium, which are widely considered by various governments as "critical materials (or critical metals)" because of their high technological importance as well as intensifying supply risks.

Consequently, the physical basis of the energy system will rapidly shift from carbon to metal (from coal and oil to rare earth, or lithium, etc.). Meanwhile, the energy sector can be expected to dominate the global markets for these metals, and the IEA's assessment indicates that the annual demand for rare earths, lithium, cobalt, and nickel from 2020 to 2040, depending on material category, will expand by 7–42-fold. This will increase further under a continued population, and affluence increase. However, most of these metals are geologically rare, scarce, and scattered, and their production capacities are difficult to quickly expand. In this context, this huge metal demand gap will make it difficult, if not impossible, for the energy system to reach an ambitious carbon-neutral target.

Such metal constraints on energy transition can become severe at the national level, because critical metals are not equally distributed and produced among nations. China stands out as the largest global low-carbon technology manufacturer with ambitious climate plans. Fig. 1b presents our preliminary analysis of China's future critical metal demand in line with its carbon-neutral target. The details of the data source and quantification methods can be found in the Supporting Material, which indicates that the energy transition in China will require an approximately 8.6-fold increase in its consumption of over 20 types of critical metals, rising from 590 thousand tons (kt)/year by 2020 to 5106 kt/year by 2040. For specialty metals, a much higher growth rate is anticipated (e.g., 18-fold for lithium, 25-fold for cobalt, 7-fold for gallium, 11-fold for neodymium, and 5-fold for platinum). As one of the world's largest critical metal suppliers, Chinese production capacities alone cannot meet demand at such a scale. Consequently, it has become the largest importer of various critical metals, even rare earths. Thus, the transition to a low-carbon energy system will not be possible without countries along the metal supply chain cooperating more effectively.

3. Metals Supply Dependence on Energy

Energy is needed at all stages of the metal life cycle, particularly in the production stages from mining to refinery (pyrometallurgical and hydrometallurgical). Currently, the energy required to produce metals is extremely carbon-intensive because it is derived mostly from coal and other fuels. In addition, the carbon obtained from these fuels, as a reductive agent and feedstock, has been integral for some long-lived chemical and metallurgical processes, meaning that a simple shift of the energy carrier is not sufficient. Thus, metal production is among the sectors that are the most challenging to decarbonize and require significant mitigation efforts. Moreover, most metals and their related products are consumed at an accelerated rate, which is expected to grow further because easy-to-mine deposits are being exploited quickly, and their demand is on the rise.

More directly, various critical metals are directly produced from fossil fuels as by-products or from host minerals, whose supply is governed by fossil fuel supply chains. There is evidence that approximately 40% of germanium, 10% of vanadium,

36% of silver, and other elements such as gallium and rare earths are associated with fossil fuel extraction . Thus, transitioning to a carbon-neutral energy system would not only increase metal demand, but may also weaken the supply of some critical metals. Without acknowledging such interdependencies, stricter climate policies (e.g., China's dual energy control policy) may further constrain metal production with higher energy costs and limited energy availability.

Nevertheless, the pathways of the metal and energy transitions are not well harmonized. Current low-carbon pathways of energy systems are mainly focused on expanding renewables, electrification, storage, and coal(fuel) phasing-out. However, material industries that require high-temperature heat with significant process emissions may not be decarbonized based on predominant approaches. Additionally, industrial production processes are highly integrated; therefore, any change in one part of the process must be accompanied by changes in other parts. Industrial facilities have relatively long lifespans (up to 50 years), thereby making decarbonization costly. Without more efforts in steering energy transition towards material needs, the continued high levels of material production will induce a rapid increase in total energy demand, most of which will remain as fuel or hard-to-decarbonated emissions by 2050.

4. Towards a Circular Metal-energy Nexus

A carbon-neutral energy system (or carbon-neutral metal system) cannot be achieved separately, and a nexus-based understanding is urgently needed. The circular economy (CE) is a holistic vision for responding to these requirements simultaneously. It includes various strategies, such as better recycling, remanufacturing, and reuse, to ensure that products, materials, and components are of the highest utility and value at all times. Here, we propose a circular metal-energy nexus (C-MEN) to encourage the global implementation of CE strategies for the amplification of metal-energy services to provide various societal services towards carbon neutrality. As shown in Fig. 2, this C-MEN framework contains three key linkages: (a) the demand for carbon-neutral metals and energy to provide carbon-neutral services (i.e., habitation, mobility, communication, etc.); (b) the need for the carbon-neutral transition of both metal and energy systems by themselves for GHG reduction; (c) the implementation of CE to promote such carbon-neutral transition of energy, metal, and their joint system as a whole.

Such a C-MEN framework can directly benefit the direct decarbonization of energy and metal systems as follows: First, it can help reduce critical metal demand ("less metal for more energy") through strategies such as material efficiency design, lifetime extension, service efficiency, and shared economy. In addition, circular flows can reduce energy needs, and the development of a CE system for material reuse and recycling can accelerate renewable integration, particularly in hard-to-decarbonize sectors (e.g., 80% of that for steel production. A shift to secondary metals may allow a greater percentage of the entire material system to be electrified from renewables. Meanwhile, under CE guidance, some new models, such as the sharing economy, industrial symbiosis, and lightweight design, may significantly affect the supply and demand of energy as well as metals.

By linking CE to the metal-energy nexus, the C-MEN framework can also benefit the decarbonization of other services. According to the Ellen McArthur Foundation, efforts to combat climate change through energy system transitions can only address 55% of global GHG emissions, and the remainder, including material production, can be reduced through CE strategies. In addition, CE can help regenerate natural systems to sequester more carbon from the atmosphere. In addition to protecting the environment, C-MEN is capable of providing financial benefits. For instance, strategies such as reusing, restoring, and remarketing modules, products, and components can help manufacturers minimize costs, increase profits, and enhance competitiveness. In turn, this could attract higher investments and accelerate the move towards renewables.

In most cases, however, this CE-based thinking is not covered or perceived as an afterthought for low-carbon technology manufacturers. At present, massive quantities of critical metals and composites are being extracted, processed, and deployed in increasingly complex low-carbon technologies, yet there is no evidence that they are designed to be disassembled, recovered, and returned to the material and product value chain. If low-carbon infrastructure is not properly managed, waste crisis is inevitable (Fig. 1b). According to our estimates (Supporting Material), the market for recovered materials from low-carbon energy products alone could total $121 million by 2030 and $32 billion by 2040 in China. Nevertheless, if present low recycling rates continue, the retired battery waste, wind turbine blades, and solar panel modules instead could increase with an annual compound rate of 135% from 9.2 thousand tons to 3.96 million tons by 2040. Thus, a joint research-business-government effort under the C-MEN framework is required, as highlighted in Fig. 2.

5. Concluding Remarks and Global Efforts

There is not much time to reverse the trend of ever-increasing GHG emissions. For a carbon-neutral future, all relevant stakeholders along the material and energy supply chains must work together to manage synergies and to plan their priorities. Material circularity at the global level can notably facilitate achieving energy transitions and climate targets. Globally coordinated efforts, such as technology transfer and emissions trading for material-intensive supply chains, are urgently needed because the climate crisis is a global challenge, and raw materials and low-carbon technologies are widely traded products in the international market.

Three global actions are proposed here to leverage such a circular metal-energy nexus (Fig. 2): first, a global organization that compiles CE energy knowledge and solutions from research and different international organizations (e.g., IEA, UNEP, IPCC) needs to be established and spreads to policymakers and businesses across the globe to provide a set of new analytical tools, policies, and approaches that support fully circular and carbon-neutral economies. In particular, the International Resource Panel (IRP) of the UNEP is a good candidate for this linkage. Second, a global CE platform is needed to promote cooperation and reduce conflicts among sectors and regions with respect to critical metal and renewable sources. The EU's proposal for a "Global Circular Economy Alliance" can be incorporated into climate agreements for this purpose. Under such an alliance, some policy mandates (e.g., recycling standards and material choice regulations) and joint grants can be used to make early investments in the circular design and treatment of low-carbon products. Finally, we need to build a global business coalition composed of major mining, metallurgical, material, renewable energy, electric vehicles and batteries, finance, and waste management companies, which can act as the main promoters to ensure a low-carbon, circular, and stable international supply chain of metals and energy.

(Adapted from "Carbon Neutrality Needs a Circular Metal-energy Nexus" by P. Wang et al in *Fundamental Research*, *2*(3), 2022.)

II. Read the following review article and make an evaluation on the structure.

The Pleasures Evoked by Taste and Olfaction

Genetic approaches to flavor improvement have proven to be very challenging, in large part due to the complexity of assessing the phenotype. The palatability of fruits and vegetables can best be understood by an examination of the components of flavor. While appearance, texture, and chemesthesis (e.g., irritation) make important contributions, the core contributors to flavor are taste and olfaction. The taste qualities, sweet, salty, sour, and bitter, have been considered "basic tastes" since the 19th century. Some experts choose to add other oral sensations to the list (e.g., metallic, fatty, umami); however, the key feature in comparisons of taste and olfaction is that the number of distinct taste qualities is small compared to the huge number of distinct olfactory qualities.

Understanding the role of olfaction in flavor requires a distinction between ortho and retronasal olfaction. Sniffing draws odorants into the nose through the nostrils where it passes over the turbinate bones (which add turbulence to the air flow); the sample then rises to the top of the nasal cavity and contacts olfactory receptors in the olfactory mucosa—this is called orthonasal olfaction (smell). Odorants emitted from foods in the mouth are forced upwards, behind the palate and into the nasal cavity from the rear by chewing and swallowing—this is called retronasal olfaction. The ultimate sensation of flavor results from the central integration of taste and retronasal olfaction.

Although retro-and orthonasal olfaction have long been known to have different properties, the proof that the brain processes them in different areas was only demonstrated relatively and recently by fMRI studies; taste and retro-nasal olfaction presumably are integrated to produce flavor at the brain locations where these inputs converge. The pleasures evoked by taste and olfaction follow different rules, making understanding the pleasure evoked by the flavors of fruits particularly interesting.

The pleasure evoked by taste is hard-wired in the brain. Newborn infants make faces consistent with pleasure to sweet and displeasure to bitter. In fact, sweet receptors are present prior to birth—injection of saccharin into amniotic fluid will induce a fetus to swallow, suggesting that sweet is affectively positive even before birth. Hard-wired affect for taste makes biological sense; the pleasure associated with food-associated sugars and dilute NaCl ensure intake of these critical nutrients. On the other hand, the displeasure associated with bitter protects from poisons.

The pleasure of olfaction is widely believed to be largely, if not entirely, learned, and this learning has biological importance. Odors paired with benefit (e.g., calories) come to be liked, while odors paired with illness (particularly nausea) come to be disliked. Although it is clear that olfactory affect is easily learned, is there any evidence that some odor-ants evoke affect that is hard-wired? Some studies on human infants and young children (1–2 years old) show that they can discriminate among odorants, but they do not show the affective responses (preference or rejection) characteristic of adults. As children grow, they begin to show preferences similar to those shown by adults. This makes biological sense, since the plasticity of olfactory pleasure allows an organism to adapt to its environment by learning to like/dislike odors based on the consequences associated with those odors. However, some investigators argue that difficulties testing infants and young children limit the conclusions that olfactory affect is entirely learned, and take the position that some odors may be "inherently pleasant or unpleasant".

While there is no evidence for innate olfactory affect in humans, many of the most important flavor-associated volatiles in fruits are derived from essential nutrients. It would clearly be biologically wise if these cues for nutritional quality had hard-wired affect. In this context, it is interesting to examine comments by Aristotle made in *On Sense and the Sensible* describing two groups of odors. The first group is associated with foods whose pleasantness is associated with nutrition. The pleasure evoked from odors in Aristotle's first group sounds remarkably like conditioned references. The second group of odors, restricted to humans, is "agreeable in their essential nature, e.g., those of flowers". Could the pleasure of Aristotle's second group (e.g., flowers) represent hard-wired olfactory affect evoked by volatiles that are cues for essential nutrients? It is provocative that the volatiles identified as cues to nutrients tend to be described as floral. This is an area that deserves further study.

The hedonic properties of flavors do not simply reflect the hard-wired affect of taste and the learned affect of olfaction. "Evaluative conditioning" refers to the fact that neutral stimuli can take on affect when they are paired with stimuli that have edonic properties (either positive or negative). This is relevant to the hedonic properties of flavors since neutral olfactory components may be rendered hedonically positive by association with sweet taste. Thus, the palatability of fruits consists not only of the palatability contributed hard-wired taste affect (e.g., sweet) and the learned affect (association of odors with calories), but also by the palatability of odors contributed by evaluative conditioning.

(Adapted from "Better Fruits and Vegetables Through Sensory Analysis" by L. M. Bartoshuk & H. J. Klee in *Current Biology, 23*(9), 2013.)

III. **Read the following statements on writing review articles and decide whether they are true (T) or false (F). Then give your reasons.**

(1) In order to demonstrate the recent development in the existing area, review articles analyze the past papers on the chosen topic.

(2) The analytical results will help lead to the new synthesis.

(3) It is always important to extend your research when you may have gathered a lot of data.

(4) The whole article is basically the answer to the research question, that is, the solution to the problem you presented at the beginning.

(5) The content of the review article should be precise, concise and can summarize the central content of the full text.

IV. **Translate the following Chinese sentences into English using the appropriate expressions chosen from the box.**

- recent research suggests...
- consider the newly identified...
- experts note that...
- in combination with...
- previous studies have indicated...
- to our knowledge

> - the overall structure of...is very similar to the previously reported structure of...
> - not yet proven...

(1) 近期的研究表明，最糟糕的一种情况是，随着全球温室气体的大量排放和人口的高速增长，接触到这种蚊子的人口可能将增加一倍，从目前的 40 亿左右增加到本世纪末的 80 亿或 90 亿。

_____

_____

(2) 人们怀疑气候变化是人类感染一系列疾病的一个主要原因，尽管这一点尚未得到证实。

_____

_____

(3) 专家在访谈中指出，没有任何一种传染病是仅由一个变量引起的。

_____

_____

(4) 先前的研究表明，吃巧克力有增加患心脏病的可能性。

_____

_____

(5) 人工智能越来越多地与实物监测结合起来使用。

_____

_____

📖 Project

Work in groups. Choose 3–4 journal review articles from different authoritative international journals in your discipline and discuss the wording, style, and organization of the review articles. Prepare a presentation to be delivered in class.

Unit 7

Responses to Reviewers' Comments and Editors' Decisions

Part I
Introducing the Unit

After submitting our manuscript to a journal, we are most likely to receive the decisions, either favorable or unfavorable, from the editors and the comments from the reviewers. There are mainly two outcomes of the decision process, i.e., being rejected and being likely to be accepted after adequate responses to the comments of the reviewers. The core task of the latter is to make major or minor revisions. At this point, a timely, clear, compelling, and well-crafted response document will increase the potential of acceptance of the revised version. In addition, most of time we may need to write a separate letter to the editors where we need to address the conflicts of interest between the reviewers and us.

In this unit, we are going to learn about some rules and techniques, in terms of structure, content, language use, and do's and don'ts, of how to write effective response letters to reviewers' comments and editors' decisions.

After finishing this unit, you are expected to achieve the following learning objectives:

- to comprehend the bits of essential information in the decision letters and the reviewers' comments;
- to revise the manuscript according to the reviewers' comments ;
- to use effective expressions in writing response letters to the reviewers' comments in a well-organized way.

Unit 7 Responses to Reviewers' Comments and Editors' Decisions

Part II
Learning Useful Expressions

Study the bold-faced expressions that are often used in responses to reviewers' comments and editors' decisions.

A. Showing Gratitude and Articulating What Has Been Done in General

- **Thank you for your kind comments on** our manuscript entitled "XXX". We **have carefully revised the manuscript** according to the reviewers' comments. Based on the suggestions, we **have made an extensive modification on** the revised manuscript. **Detailed revision** was shown as follows.

- **Thank you for your nice comments on** our article. According to your suggestions, we **have supplemented some data** here and **corrected several mistakes** in our previous draft. Based on your comments, we also **attached a point-by-point letter** to you and the other two reviewers. We have **made extensive revisions to** our previous draft. The detailed point-by-point responses are listed below.

- **Thank you for** your e-mail dated 21/07/2021 enclosing the reviewers' comments. We **have carefully reviewed the comments and have revised the manuscript** accordingly. Our responses are given **in a point-by-point manner** below.

- We **thank reviewers for** their constructive criticism, and time spent to analyze this manuscript. The **responses and explanations** related to their comments are listed below.

- We **are very grateful to** your comments and thoughtful suggestions. In the revised manuscript, we **have modified** the picture drawn in Scheme 4 (original Scheme 5).

- On behalf of all the contributing authors, I would like to **express our sincere appreciations of** your letter and the reviewers' constructive comments concerning our article entitled "XXX" (Manuscript No.: XXX). These comments are all **valuable** and **helpful** for improving our article.

- I **greatly appreciate the time and effort** you've put into your comments. Your advice about the formatting, structure, and referencing style of my paper is **most helpful**.

B. Specifying the Changes and Their Presenting Forms

- According to the associate editor and reviewers' comments, we have made extensive modifications to our manuscript and **supplemented extra data** to make our results convincing.
- In this revised version, changes to our manuscript were all **highlighted** within the document **by using red colored text**.
- **According to your suggestion, we have removed** the imido section and **re-written the manuscript focusing on** the sulfido and oxo complexes.
- I have **responded specifically to** each suggestion below, beginning with your own. To make the changes easier to identify where necessary, I have **numbered** them.
- Changes to the manuscript are shown **in underline/red/bold**.

C. Showing Agreement and Disagreement

- We **agree with** the reviewer. In respond to this comment and to a comment raised by the other reviewer, we have revised the text as follows.
- **We agree with the reviewer's comments concerning this issue. However,** we indeed have provided these reactions in the original Supporting Information, such as Page S19 Line 11 (Method C), Page 20 Line 11 (Method B).

Part III
Learning Ways of Organization

In this part, we are going to discuss the structures and contents of the response documents so as to develop the skills of writing response letters to reviewers' comments and editors' decisions for academic papers in science and technology.

Writing Effective Responses to Reviewers' Comments

An effective "response to reviewers" document, summarizing the changes that the authors made in response to the comments, is submitted alongside with the revised manuscript. Failure to spend time elaborating the document but focusing on revising the manuscript itself may produce misunderstandings between the reviewers

Unit 7 Responses to Reviewers' Comments and Editors' Decisions

and the authors, and lead to the possible rejection of a potentially high-quality manuscript. To formulate an effective response to reviewers, we need to go through the following three stages.

Stage 1: A Thorough Understanding of the Reviewers' Comments and Editors' Decision Letters

- We need to carefully read the accompanying letter from the editors to find out what has been highlighted in the reviewers' comments, and whether any extra points have been proposed.
- We need to carefully read the reviewers' comments and check the points listed by the reviewers with the manuscript.
- We need to carefully discuss the comments, and our reply (and the details of additional experiments) with the co-authors to decide to what extent we need to revise the manuscript based on the reviewers' comments.

Stage 2: A Point-to-point Reply to the Reviewers' Comments

A clear and logical structure helps the editors and reviewers to see what the authors have revised and to ensure that any point addressed by the journal is included.

Every page needs a heading with "Reply to the comments on manuscript [title of the manuscript] [manuscript ID number]" and "[the author's name] et al."

The response document needs an introduction, summarizing major changes the authors have made, either as one part of the document or in a separate cover letter to the editors. Gratitude also needs to be expressed in this part to the editors and reviewers for their efforts.

The response document should be arranged in the following way: We should first copy and paste the comments or questions, or offer a short summary of the point picked up. If the comments are not numbered, we need to divide them into individual comments. We can use italics or bolds to highlight the comments. For instance:

> **Comment 1** (*for comment 1 from reviewer 1*)
>
> **Reply 1** (*the reply to comment 1 from reviewer 1*)
>
> **Comment 2**
>
> **Reply 2**
>
> **Comment 3**

Reply 3

...

This document can also be used as the framework or the "to-do-list" in the early phase to outline how the authors are going to deal with the comments. In the beginning, we can simply type some keywords of the ideas about the revision or attempt to add experiments or evaluation where appropriate. As the progress goes on, we can modify these ideas when necessary.

In addition to a reasonable framework and structure, the content of the reply plays an important role in the future possible acceptance. The following negligible details make a great contribution:

- Keep the internal communication smooth. We need to discuss with the co-authors about the comments thoroughly before doing anything and always exchange the proposed reply with them before submission. Their comments and suggestions greatly help improve the quality of the reply, and we are supposed to reply as a team.
- Stick to the requirements of the journal. The requirements from different journals for submitting a revised version may vary greatly.
- Show respect for reviewers and editors. The reviewers spend their valuable time working on these research papers. Sometimes they appear to make "stupid" comments and we may feel that "they have not understood my paper", but this could also mean that the readers of our manuscript have not understood what we want to say.
- Focus on the details while including all. We should always be specific in the response and touch on all the points identified:
  - For the comment on a spelling error, we can answer "This has now been amended", "We agree", or "We apologize for this omission".
  - For the point raised by more than one reviewer, we can answer "This point has been addressed in the reply to comment x of reviewer y".
  - For the point that we cannot address, we should explain why.
  - For the comment that we feel is outside the scope of our study, we should explain why.
  - For any point that we do not agree with the reviewer, such as the suggested additional experiment or analysis that we think is not needed,

we should explain why.
- ➢ For any change that we have not made, we should not claim to have done so.
- Eliminate anything redundant. If any part of the manuscript has been required to be cut, we should do so. We can even make it clear by stating how many words or how large a percentage we have shortened it.
- Mark when making changes. We should always show where we have made a change in the manuscript in response to the comments: "This is now addressed in the Discussion section of the revised manuscript on Page x, Line y."
- Address in the third person. The response is written to the editors rather than the reviewers so that we should refer to the reviewers in the third person, such as "We agree with the reviewer…" rather than "We agree with you…".

Stage 3: A Careful Language Editing

If time permits, we had better write our response document twice. The draft of the document focuses on the analysis of what the reviewers meant and simultaneously considers different paths of responses and the cost of performing additional experiments. Then we can begin writing what we want the reviewers to read. Every point in the response document should target the point raised by the reviewers. The editing work also works at this stage, involving word selection, grammar, and the style of the manuscript.

Writing Appropriate Responses to Editors' Decisions

It is good news that we receive an e-mail saying that the manuscript is nice but not acceptable as it is. Actually, few manuscripts are accepted without any revision and this merely indicates that the journal is interested in our manuscript. Thus, besides the "response to reviewers" document, we may need to write a letter to the editors, in which we can address the issues about potential conflicts of interest, the reviewers' requests conflicting with one another or with journal policies, etc.

When Receiving a Rejection with Peer Review Reports

We need to be clear that the reviewers' comments are the major reference for the editors' decision rather than the only criterion. The manuscript's suitability for the journal, statistical reliability, general interest, and novelty are also taken into account.

When we feel that the reviewers or editors have not understood our work or have misunderstood our paper, we can contact the journal for clarification or submit a formal rebuttal.

Composing a rebuttal letter entails a professional approach rather than an emotional or sensational one, which clarifies the reasons for challenging the decision.

When Receiving a "Revise" Decision with Requests from Reviewers

Some of the requests may be conflicting, or require what we think is not feasible or appropriate. In this case, it is fine for us not to do as required and it is necessary to prepare a point-by-point response to these requests and explain our reasons in the response document.

It should also be kept in mind that anything uploaded is what we want the reviewers and editors to read, especially the wording of the response to critical comments or where we disagree or agree with the reviewers. For open peer review adopted by some journals, if the paper is accepted, the response document will be published online as well.

There is still another possibility: The paper is rejected before peer review. Most likely, the manuscript is not in the scope of the journal, or too specialized, or just unsuitable. In this case, we had better turn to another journal as some editors may suggest a more suitable journal in their decision letters or offer to transfer the manuscript to another journal (of the same publishing house).

To sum up, the responses to the reviewers' comments and the editors' decisions are supposed to keep the communication between the reviewers and editors, and the authors positive and productive. Good responses are short, direct, and to the point. The authors need to address and number every single comment. They may accept blame, or explain why they have not made changes as instructed if they think they need to do so, or highlight what and where new material is. But the authors should not ignore the comments that they have no idea how to handle or the comments they cannot understand, or pretend to have dealt with a comment when they really did not.

Unit 7 Responses to Reviewers' Comments and Editors' Decisions

Part IV
Analyzing an Example

In this part, we are going to analyze an example so as to understand the wording, structures, and moves of responses to reviewers' comments and editors' decisions for academic papers in science and technology.

Analyze the following response letter to both the editor's decisions and the reviewers' comments, and discuss the questions with a partner.

Prof. Dr. XXX

Associate Editor

Journal of XXX

E-mail: XXX@XXX.XXX.org

RE: Manuscript ID: XXX

Title: "XXX"

Author(s): XXX

Dear Professor XXX,

Thank you for your consideration of our manuscript entitled "XXX" for publication in *Journal of XXX*.

According to your and the reviewers' comments, we have revised the manuscript. The comments are constructive and the suggested changes have made the manuscript a better paper. These changes are described below in detail. For your use, a copy of the manuscript containing annotation where changes were made (noted in yellow) is also uploaded as a "Supporting Information for Review Only" file.

Thank you for your gracious handling of our submission.

With kind regards,

XXX

List of Changes

We outline below the changes we have made to the manuscript and the reasons for the changes.

Response to Manuscript Revision Request—Non-scientific Changes

Comments:

1. If possible, please update the status of Reference 5e.

Response: The status of Reference 9e (original 5e) has been updated.

2. Please make sure to correct the title so it matches on the Manuscript file, Supporting Information and Paragon plus submitting page.

Response: The title on the Manuscript file, Supporting Information and Paragon plus submitting page has been corrected to "An Actinide Metallacyclopropene Complex: Synthesis, Structure, Reactivity, and Computational Studies".

3. Please make sure to remove the author list and manuscript title from TOC graphic.

Response: The author list and manuscript title have been removed from TOC graphic.

Response to Reviewer 1

Comment 1: The thorium chemistry described in the enclosed manuscript details the synthesis, characterization, and reactivity of a thorium metallacyclopropene complex. The synthesis and characterization of all complexes was performed very thoroughly, as shown by inclusion of both the prep scale and NMR tube reactions. The identities of the compounds are all clearly established, and there is no doubt as to the interpretation.

In reading this manuscript, I was surprised by the lack of broad discussion, given that this manuscript has been submitted to XXX. While the authors conclude that the metallacyclopropene acts "resembles more closely an actinide metal than a d-transition metal" (which most would have guessed), more discussion on the classical transition metal systems would have been expected. The metallacyclopropene gives the authors an opportunity to discuss some long-standing

Unit 7 Responses to Reviewers' Comments and Editors' Decisions

issues in actinide chemistry, and no such discussion is present.

For instance, it would have been effective to include in the introduction a specific mention of the Dewar-Chatt model, which describes the differences in bonding between the two possible resonance forms—the n2-alkyne or the metallacyclopropene—for the broad audience. There was a bonding discussion based on X-ray parameters and DFT, which was helpful, but introducing the ideas earlier would allow the readers to frame these results. Also missing was a discussion of the vast transition metal literature that attempts to classify such compounds based on their characterization and reactivity. There was also not a discussion of the metrical parameters of the alkyne ligand for the thorium compound as compared to Group 4 derivatives. The magnetic data do contribute to this discussion, which was helpful in terms of assigning the oxidation state, by which ligand oxidation state was then inferred.

Response 1: The introduction of the Dewar-Chatt model has been added into the "Introduction", that is, the sentences "The bonding in these complexes can be rationalized by the Dewar-Chatt-Duncanson model, that was originally introduced to describe the bonding in metal olefin complexes, but can be extended to metal alkyne complexes. Within this model the bonding in metallacyclopropenes can be described by two extreme resonance structures, that are, ϖ-complex (A) and metallacyclopropene (B) (Figure 1). While, in both cases the alkyne acts as a 2-electron donor ligand, the difference between the resonance structures A and B arises from extend of ϖ-back-bonding which occurs between the metal atom and the alkyne ligand. Furthermore, for electron-poor fragments the alkyne can act as additional ϖ-donor ligand providing electron density for the metal atom via the orthogonal ϖ-system and therefore acting as a 4-electron donor ligand (Figure 1, C). On molecular orbital (MO) level, these interactions can be described by combining MOs of the metal fragment with those alkyne ϖ-MOs of proper symmetry (Figure 1)". And Figure 1 and related references (Ref. 8–10) have been added into the revision.

Moreover, a discussion of the transition metal literature that attempts to classify such compounds based on their characterization and reactivity has been added; for example, the sentences such as "Late (and electron rich) transition metals (such as Pt, Pd, Ni, Co) are known for their ability to undergo strong M→alkyne ϖ-back-donation, and have been used extensively in organic synthesis, e.g., mediating a variety of organic transformations such as cyclotrimerization of alkynes, preparation of pyridines and cyclopentadienones from alkynes and isonitriles, olefins, or carbon monoxide. In contrast, ϖ-back-bonding is weaker in actinides metals, but becomes relevant, for example, to explain the bonding in the U(III) complex $(Me_3SiC_5H_4)_3U(CO)$", and related references (Ref. 4 and 11) have been added into the revision.

In addition, a discussion of the metrical parameters of the alkyne ligand for the thorium compound as compared to Group 4 derivatives has been added, that is, the sentence "The relevant $C(18)-C(18A)$ distance of 1.343(4) Å is significantly longer than that of the free PhC≡CPh molecule (1.210(3) Å) and much closer to the value of a typical double bond (1.331 Å) and comparable to those found in Group 4 metallacyclopropenes" has been added into the revision.

Comment 2: The view by most chemists is that actinides participate in back-bonding to a very small extent as compared to transition metals, which is of course the fundamental concept prevailing in the Dewar-Chatt model for transition metals. Clearly, back-bonding is at play in the identification of the metallacyclopropene product; yet this is not mentioned specifically. Why does back-bonding occur here when actinides aren't typically shown to undergo such behavior? This discussion is of course related to the lack of actinide carbonyl complexes as compared to their transition metal congeners, which is also never discussed. It also seems appropriate to include a brief (1–2 sentences) discussion of the previously reported actinide metallacyclopropenes that are mentioned in Reference 6 in the introduction to frame the results for the readers. For publication in such a broad journal, it seems like the authors should be showing how this unique compound contributes to the overall understanding of the f block and how its chemistry differs from the d block.

Response 2: Some discussions on back-bonding in the identification of the metallacyclopropene product have been added; for example, the sentences "Next, the exchange of diphenylacetylene with MeC≡CMe, PhC≡CMe, and (*p*-tolyl)C≡C(*p*-tolyl) was investigated at elevated temperatures on a chemical time scale, but no exchange was observed in contrast to Group 4 metallacyclopropene complexes. From these observations complex **2** is better described as a thorium metallacyclopropene

Unit 7 Responses to Reviewers' Comments and Editors' Decisions

(Th(IV) with a [η²-alkenediyl]²⁻ ligand than a thorium(II) ϖ-alkyne complex (Figure 1)" have been added into the revision.

Some discussions on back-bonding in different behaviors between actinides and transition metals have been added; for example, the sentences "Late (and electron rich) transition metals (such as Pt, Pd, Ni, Co) are known for their ability to undergo strong M→alkyne ϖ-back-donation", "In contrast, ϖ-back-bonding is weaker in actinides metals, but becomes relevant, for example, to explain the bonding in the U(III) complex $(Me_3SiC_5H_4)_3U(CO)$", and "Most notably, while the ϖ-U(III) alkyne complex $(\eta^5-C_5H_5)_3U(\eta^2-PhC\equiv CPh)$ was spectroscopically observed, it exhibited only limited stability, which presumably originates from a the weaker M→alkyne ϖ-back-bonding in this U(III) complex when compared to d-transition metal complexes" and the related references (Ref. 4, 10, and 11) have been added into the revision.

Comment 3: There were a number of typographical and grammatical errors that need to be addressed.

Response 3: Typos or grammatical errors have been corrected.

Comment 4: The reactivity displayed by these complexes is clearly interesting. Many of the products have not been previously observed. The authors did a nice job of characterizing resulting products. Additionally, there were extensive computational discussions of how the various reactions proceed, identifying the key intermediates and transition states. The figures labeled are effective in conveying these complex schemes as well. While this was helpful to the understanding, there wasn't a lot of experimental support for the computational findings, which detracted from the overall story.

Response 4: We have tried many reactions, but some intermediates are very active, which cannot be isolated.

Comment 5: The conclusion reads like a summary of the abstract. Further explanations about the character of the metallacyclopropene as well as its contribution to understanding the organometallic chemistry as compared to transition metals would end the story nicely.

Response 5: Some discussions about the character of the metallacyclopropene as well as its contribution to understanding the organometallic chemistry as compared to transition metals have been added into the "Conclusions"; for example, the sentences such as "Density functional theory (DFT) shows that 5f orbitals contribute to the σ-bond of the Th-(η^2-C=C) moiety, and also very polarized bonds are found between the [η^5-1,2,4-(Me$_3$C)$_3$C$_5$H$_2$]$_2$Th^{2+} and the [PhC=CPh]$^{2-}$ fragments" and "Furthermore, while the alkyne moieties in the more covalent Group 4 metallacyclopropenes are readily exchanged with alkynes and carbodiimides, this is not the case in thorium complex **2**" have been provided. In addition, we end the story in this comparison.

Response to Reviewer 2

Comments:

Accordingly, I very much recommend this manuscript for publication in XXX with the few, very minor revisions noted below.

1. Although the general conciseness of the manuscript is much appreciated, this reviewer would welcome a brief discussion of the literature-known examples of actinide cyclopropenes, and their reactivity. Even though their molecular structures are unknown, careful spectroscopic characterization—at least in the case of Ephritikhine's [Cp$_3$U(PhCCPh)]—provides evidence for the proposed metallacyclopropene. A general reference to the actinide-mediated activation of alkenes and alkynes, recently reviewed in *Prog. Inorg. Chem.* (2014, Vol.58), might be useful as well.

Response: A brief discussion of the literature-known example of actinide cyclopropenes has been added; for example, the sentences "Most notably, while the ϖ-U(III) alkyne complex (η^5-C$_5$H$_5$)$_3$U(η^2-PhC≡CPh) was spectroscopically observed, it exhibited only limited stability, which presumably originates from a the weaker M→alkyne ϖ-back-bonding in this U(III) complex when compared to d-transition metal complexes" and "In contrast to ϖ-U(III) alkyne complex (η^5-C$_5$H$_5$)$_3$U(PhC≡CPh), variable-temperature (20℃–100℃) ^{1}H NMR investigations reveal that no dissociation of complex **2** occurs when it is heated to 100℃…" have been added into the revision. The reference *Prog. Inorg. Chem.* (2014, Vol.58, 303–415) has been cited (see Ref. 6).

2. The Th-C distance within the metallacyclopropene is reported at 2.395(2) Å.

Unit 7   Responses to Reviewers' Comments and Editors' Decisions

The authors state that this distance "is shorter than the reported Th-C(sp^2) sigma-bonds 2.420(3)–2.654(14) Å". This statement is correct, but barely. Within the 3-sigma criterion, the shortest of the given examples is just barely shorter than the one found in complex **2**. Perhaps the authors could tone down this statement a little?

Response: The sentence has been revised to "The distance Th-C(18) or Th-C(18A) of 2.395(2) Å is on the lower end of the reported Th-C(sp^2) σ-bonds (2.420(3)–2.654(14) Å)".

3. On Page 5, bottom, the authors state that "Th^{4+} resembles more closely an actinide metal than a d-transition metal". Thorium is an actinide metal! This sentence should be deleted and the following sentence re-phrased. Prior to this sentence, the authors clearly and sufficiently state, "From these results a metallacyclopropene moiety with a delocalized aromatic system as described for Group 4 complexes can be discounted."

Response: The sentence "Th^{4+} resembles more closely an actinide metal than a d-transition metal" has been removed, and the following sentence has been revised to "This agrees with the experimental findings that the alkyne moiety in the more covalent Group 4 metallacyclopropene complexes can readily be replaced by other alkynes, whereas no exchange is observed in thorium complex **2**".

4. The reactivity studies of complex **2** towards the variety of substrates ought to find a place in the "Conclusions". Thus, this reviewer would appreciate a brief, generalized summary of the presented reactivity studies within the "Conclusions" part.

Response: A brief generalized summary of the presented reactivity studies has been added into the "Conclusions"; for example, the sentence "as illustrated by its reaction with hetero-unsaturated molecules such as aldehydes, ketones, carbodiimide, nitriles, organic azides, and diazoalkane derivatives, leading to five-membered metallaheterocycles or rearranged products" has been added into the revision.

Response to Reviewer 3

Comments:

Page 1: The synthesis of complex **2** goes over a Th(III) intermediate, as the Th(IV)Cl$_2$ precursor is reduced with KC$_8$. Was the reaction followed by ESR? Since there are not many examples of Th(III) complexes in the literature, it would be interesting to follow the reaction in situ by NMR and ESR, if the authors have the possibility to perform ESR measurements at low temperatures.

Response: Yes, the reaction was followed by NMR and ESR, but no Th(III) complex was detected.

Page 1: Can the thorium metallacyclopropene be synthesized for other R substituents on the acetylene, such as non-aromatic substituents? Or is the reaction limited to diphenylacetylene?

Response: The thorium metallacyclopropene can be synthesized for other R substituents on the acetylene, even for non-aromatic substituents. This result will be reported in due course.

Page 8: If the thorium pinacolate complex is only formed because of the steric hindrance of the diphenylketone, then this reaction could be performed with a less sterically hindered ketone, e.g., dimethyl ketone, or phenyl methyl ketone. The comparison of the diphenylketone with the p-choloro aldehyde is in my opinion not correct, because the substrates display also different electronic properties. Moreover, the reactivity of aldehydes vs ketones is known to be different (e.g., Tishchenko reaction with ketones doesn't work). Therefore, I think the reaction with MeCOMe and MeCOPh should be added.

Response: We have tried the reactions of complex **2** with ketones bearing α-Hsuch as MeCOMe and MeCOPh; in these reactions the complex **2** degraded because the deprotonation reaction occurs.

Page 8: Has the reaction been performed with only one equivalent of ketone? This could provide spectroscopic evidence for the thorium-oxo intermediate.

Response: Yes, we have tried the reaction of complex **2** with one equivalent of Ph_2CO; the resonances due to the thorium pinacolate complex **7** along with those of PhC≡CPh and unreacted complex **2** were observed by ^1H NMR spectroscopy (50% conversion based on complex **2**), but no η^2-ketone complex was detected. This information has been provided in Experimental section.

(Adapted from an anonymous real example.)

Unit 7 Responses to Reviewers' Comments and Editors' Decisions

Questions:

1. What is the structure and content of the letter to the editor?

2. How does the response document conform with the points made in Part III?

3. What attitude do the three reviewers have towards the manuscript?

Exercises

I. Read the following editor's decision letter and the reviewers' comments. Work out a workflow to respond to them.

> Dear Prof. XXX,
>
> Thank you for submitting the article "XXX" to this journal. Our impression is that the above-mentioned manuscript might indeed become suitable for publication in *Chemistry and Biodiversity*. The comments of the referees are included at the bottom of this letter.
>
> A revised version of your manuscript that takes into account the comments of the referees will be reconsidered for publication. We expect a submission of a revised version by July 22, 2020. If you feel you might need extra time, don't hesitate to contact us.
>
> Please note that submitting a revision of your manuscript does not guarantee eventual acceptance, and that your revision may be subject to re-review by the referees before a decision is rendered.
>
> 1. Please upload the manuscript file as a Microsoft Word document ("Manuscript").
>
> 2. If a "new" or "novel" compound is synthesized or isolated, the compound MUST be fully characterized. Otherwise acceptance is not possible! Please provide IR data of compounds 2 and 3!
>
> 3. References
>
> All the cited references in the text should be in square brackets [ ], in superscript and should be provided after a comma (,) or a point (.), e.g., references to book chapters, [6] books, [7] patents, [8] computer programs, [7, 8, 15] and Ph.D. theses. [10] ([6], [7, 8, 15], [5–8]…should be provided after a comma (,) or a point (.) as superscript!)

Unit 7 Responses to Reviewers' Comments and Editors' Decisions

Titles of journals must be abbreviated according to Chemical Abstracts (cf. Chemical Abstracts Service Source Index [CASSI] and provide in italics! e.g., "Organic letters" should be "*Org. Lett*".

Please provide the references according to "Instructions for Authors"!

4. NMR Multiplets / Spectroscopic Data

Please note that *Chemistry and Biodiversity* represents multiplets in the ^{1}H-NMR part as ranges as shown in this example: 4.23–4.29 (m, 2H). For all multiplets, a ppm range is required, no matter whether it is in the text or in the tables.

A doublet in NMR has one coupling constant expressed in Hertz. A triplet is the same: one coupling constant in Hertz (Hz). A doublet × doublet (dd) has per definition two coupling constants. A doublet has a single ppm value and not a ppm range.

Please provide NMR data as follows: 3.33 (t, J=4.8, H-C (2), 4 H); or 3.33 (2t, J=4.8, H-C(2), 4 H); 4.00 (dd, J=9.6, 6.0); 1.46–1.55 (m); 2.39 (t, J=8.4); 1.24 (s)…

5. Graphical Abstract

A representative structural formula, scheme, or figure should be provided for the Table of Contents. Please provide a separate TIF file with 600 dpi for your Graphical Abstract! If your Graphical Abstract containing any chemical structures or formulae, please provide separate ChemDraw file additionally! The maximum available space for this Graphical Abstract is max. 7 cm height and max. 11 cm width.

6. Graphical Material

For each figure or scheme containing any chemical structures or formulae, please provide a separate ChemDraw file (one file per Formulae collection, Figure, or Scheme). Please provide separate ChemDraw files for figures 1, 2, 3!

Additionally, please provide the separate graphic files for all figures. Please adjust the dimensions of the graphics to either one- or two-column representation. For one-column figures, the width is max. 8.19 cm, with 600 dpi resolution, for two column graphics max. 17.0 cm width, with 600 dpi resolution. Graphical files with lower resolution will lead to poor quality. If you cannot provide TIF-files, please provide the original files.

Files of the original graphics/artwork in easy-to-handle formats like ChemDraw, TIF, or EPS, or, alternatively, PDF files generated from all your vector graphics are highly welcome for print purposes.

Reviewer 1:

This paper describes the isolation and structural elucidation of three new polymethylated phloroglucinol meroterpenoids from the twigs and leaves of Rhodomyrtus tomentosa. A lot of spectroscopic data have been analyzed to prove the structures. In addition, all these isolates were evaluated for their antibacterial and AChE inhibitory activities. However, the manuscript presents some drawbacks.

1. Figure 4. The calculated ECD spectra of compounds 1–3 were not well consistent with the experimental ones.

2. The UV and IR spectra of new compounds should be provided in the Supporting Information.

3. Please show atom numbers in Figure 2.

4. Table 1. Some signals of ^{1}H NMR were presented as "m". Please note that "m" means "multiplet". If the proton signals are overlapped, it should be stated as "overlapped", not "multiplet". In other words, overlapped signals are usually reported without designating multiplicity.

5. In Experimental section, "to yield five fractions (D1–D7)" should be changed to "to yield five fractions (D1–D5)".

6. In Results and Discussion section, "Guangxi Province of China" should be changed to "Guangxi Zhuang Autonomous Region of China".

Reviewer 2:

Nice work. My truly compliments to respected authors.

Overall, this manuscript (MS) is favorably rated: 8.50 out of 10.

Recommendation: Major Changes (Major Revisions)

To be completely honest with you, the English language itself requires polishing

Unit 7 Responses to Reviewers' Comments and Editors' Decisions

at a moderate extent. Please, genially put your efforts in such a direction.

If English is polished, this highly informed MS has a real potential to be clearly recognized and truly appreciated by the members of the global academic/research community. Hopefully, it will earn a number of hetero-citations (= will be frequently cited), once when launched/published.

Therefore, I strongly encourage the authors to shortly submit the revised form of their rather promising MS to *Chemistry and Biodiversity*, Wiley Online Library.

Last but not least, very best of research luck ahead to you all.

(Adapted from an anonymous real example.)

II. Below is a complete version of the reviewers' comments on a manuscript receiving the "Rejection" decision. Read the comments carefully and list the points that need to be changed if the authors would like to publish it in the future.

View Reviews

Paper ID   XXX

Paper Title   XXX

Track Name   Main Track

Reviewer 1

Questions

1. {Summary} Please briefly summarize the main claims/contributions of the paper in your own words. (Please do not include your evaluation of the paper here.)

This paper proposes a model inversion method cGMI that can generate inversion samples by optimizing the conditional input. Compared with the existing methods, cGMI investigates the impact of classes in auxiliary datasets that could help improve the generated image quality.

2. {Novelty} How novel are the concepts, problems addressed, or methods introduced in the paper?

Fair: The paper contributes some new ideas.

3. {Soundness} Is the paper technically sound?

Good: The paper appears to be technically sound, but I have not carefully checked the details.

4. {Impact} How do you rate the likely impact of the paper on the AI research community?

Good: The paper is likely to have high impact within a subfield of AI or moderate impact across more than one subfield of AI.

5. {Clarity} Is the paper well organized and clearly written?

Good: The paper is well organized but the presentation could be improved.

6. {Evaluation} If applicable, are the main claims well supported by experiments?

Good: The experimental evaluation is adequate, and the results convincingly support the main claims.

7. {Resources} If applicable, how would you rate the new resources (code, datasets) the paper contributes? (It might help to consult the paper's reproducibility checklist.)

Fair: The shared resources are likely to be moderately useful to other AI researchers.

8. {Reproducibility} Are the results (e.g., theorems, experimental results) in the paper easily reproducible? (It may help to consult the paper's reproducibility checklist.)

Fair: Key resources (e.g., proofs, code, data) are unavailable but key details (e.g., proof sketches, experimental setup) are sufficiently well-described for an expert to confidently reproduce the main results.

9. {Ethical Considerations} Does the paper adequately address the applicable ethical considerations, e.g., responsible data collection and use (e.g., informed consent, privacy), possible societal harm (e.g., exacerbating injustice or discrimination due to algorithmic bias), etc.?

Unit 7 Responses to Reviewers' Comments and Editors' Decisions

Fair: The paper addresses some but not all of the applicable ethical considerations.

10. {Reasons to Accept} Please list the key strengths of the paper (explain and summarize your rationale for your evaluations with respect to questions 1–9 above).

The paper has investigated the impact of the auxiliary information about the target class.

11. {Reasons to Reject} Please list the key weaknesses of the paper (explain and summarize your rationale for your evaluations with respect to questions 1–9 above).

① The author should better explain the differences between the proposed method and GMI. In the Conclusion section, the authors claim that they try to reconstruct representative samples of a target class without auxiliary information about the target class. However, the authors have also stated that under the guidance of labels, we can more effectively generate samples of a target class. It is quite confusing to me whether the proposed method leverages the class/label information.

② The experiments of this paper are on toy datasets such as MNIST, which is not convincing as the GMI paper presents experimental results on face image datasets.

③ Many grammar mistakes:

- through gradually decrease its quantity (through gradually decreasing its quantity).
- Conditional Generative Model Inversion (**Conditional Generative Model Inversion** [It should be bold in the section for title consistency]).
- First, we random select 50 images from each class in the training dataset (First, we randomly select 50 images from each class in the training dataset).
- a field that completely unknown to humans (a field that is completely unknown to humans).

12. {Questions for the Authors} Please provide questions that you would like the authors to answer during the author feedback period. Please number them.

See above.

13. {Detailed Feedback for the Authors} Please provide other detailed, constructive, feedback to the authors.

See above.

14. {Overall Evaluation} Please provide your overall evaluation of the paper, carefully weighing the reasons to accept and the reasons to reject the paper. Ideally, we should have: (1) no more than 25% of the submitted papers in (Accept+Strong Accept+Very Strong Accept+Award Quality) categories; (2) no more than 20% of the submitted papers in (Strong Accept+Very Strong Accept+Award Quality) categories; (3) no more than 10% of the submitted papers in (Very Strong Accept+Award Quality) categories; (4) no more than 1% of the submitted papers in the Award Quality category.

Borderline reject: Technically solid paper where reasons to reject, e.g., lack of novelty, outweigh reasons to accept, e.g., good evaluation. Please use sparingly.

...

20. I acknowledge that I have read the authors' rebuttal and made whatever changes to my review where necessary.

Agreement accepted.

Reviewer 2

Questions

1. {Summary} Please briefly summarize the main claims/contributions of the paper in your own words. (Please do not include your evaluation of the paper here.)

The paper proposed a new adversarial attack on knowledge inversion. The method is to train a GAN on the auxiliary dataset, and then generate samples of the target class.

2. {Novelty} How novel are the concepts, problems addressed, or methods introduced in the paper?

Fair: The paper contributes some new ideas.

Unit 7 Responses to Reviewers' Comments and Editors' Decisions

3. {Soundness} Is the paper technically sound?

Fair: The paper has minor, easily fixable, technical flaws that do not impact the validity of the main results.

4. {Impact} How do you rate the likely impact of the paper on the AI research community?

Fair: The paper is likely to have moderate impact within a subfield of AI.

5. {Clarity} Is the paper well organized and clearly written?

Fair: The paper is somewhat clear, but some important details are missing or unclear.

6. {Evaluation} If applicable, are the main claims well supported by experiments?

Poor: The experimental evaluation is flawed or the results fail to adequately support the main claims.

7. {Resources} If applicable, how would you rate the new resources (code, datasets) the paper contributes? (It might help to consult the paper's reproducibility checklist.)

Fair: The shared resources are likely to be moderately useful to other AI researchers.

8. {Reproducibility} Are the results (e.g., theorems, experimental results) in the paper easily reproducible? (It may help to consult the paper's reproducibility checklist.)

Fair: Key resources (e.g., proofs, code, data) are unavailable but key details (e.g., proof sketches, experimental setup) are sufficiently well-described for an expert to confidently reproduce the main results.

9. {Ethical Considerations} Does the paper adequately address the applicable ethical considerations, e.g., responsible data collection and use (e.g., informed consent, privacy), possible societal harm (e.g., exacerbating injustice or discrimination due to algorithmic bias), etc.?

Good: The paper adequately addresses most, but not all, of the applicable ethical considerations.

10. {Reasons to Accept} Please list the key strengths of the paper (explain and summarize your rationale for your evaluations with respect to questions 1–9 above).

① The paper is well written, easy to follow.

② The paper provides enough background details on the knowledge inversion attack.

③ The paper also provides visualization results to support the claims.

④ The general framework of the knowledge inversion attack is OK.

11. {Reasons to Reject} Please list the key weaknesses of the paper (explain and summarize your rationale for your evaluations with respect to questions 1–9 above).

① One thing that concerns me the most is the robustness of the experimental results.

First, the datasets evaluated in this paper seem to be too simple, only MNIST and Fashion-MNIST, while existing works evaluate on more complicated datasets such as CIFAR-10, CelebA, as in one of the baselines (Yang et al. 2019).

Second, the proposed method is evaluated only against two works, namely, GMI and NNI; this seems too few to convince me of the advantages of the proposed method. For example, could the following attacks also be valid to compare the proposed framework with?

- Machine Learning with Membership Privacy Using Adversarial Regularization, Milad Nasr, Reza Shokri, Amir Houmansadr, 2018
- Privacy Risk in Machine Learning: Analyzing the Connection to Overfitting, S. Yeom, I. Giacomelli, M. Fredrikson, and S. Jha, 2018

Third, while the paper provides many experiments, most of them are ablation experiments, which is good but not enough given that only one experiment is performed against other comparison methods, i.e., Figure 3. How about MSE proposed in Yang et al. (2019), and attack accuracy, KNN distribution, Feature distribution in GMI (Zhang et al. 2020)? Moreover, the results in Figure 3 are confusing. Are the samples evaluated on the whole test dataset? Because from the wording, I understood that the authors randomly pick five generated samples.

Fourth, it seems to me that evaluating only one target model is not enough because the framework is an attacker, so I'd expect that the attack works against more than one target model.

② The objective function in equation 4 is a bit confusing. What if the optimally is not the same as the target class? Then, wouldn't the generated samples be completely wrong? The target model is in itself confused between two classes. For example, if the optimal y in this case is dog, should the target class be cat? Is this the reason why Figure 2b generates 1 while the target class is 6? I assume that the last row should have been the ground truth row?

③ The novelty of the framework seems limited; GMI already uses the GAN to generate target class samples. What is the difference between the proposed framework and GMI?

④ Figure 1 is confusing to understand.

12. {Questions for the Authors} Please provide questions that you would like the authors to answer during the author feedback period. Please number them.

Please address the comments above.

13. {Detailed Feedback for the Authors} Please provide other detailed, constructive, feedback to the authors.

Nothing in particular.

14. {Overall Evaluation} Please provide your overall evaluation of the paper, carefully weighing the reasons to accept and the reasons to reject the paper. Ideally, we should have: (1) no more than 25% of the submitted papers in (Accept+Strong Accept+Very Strong Accept+Award Quality) categories; (2) no more than 20% of the submitted papers in (Strong Accept+Very Strong Accept+Award Quality) categories; (3) no more than 10% of the submitted papers in (Very Strong Accept+Award Quality) categories; (4) no more than 1% of the submitted papers in the Award Quality category.

> Reject: For instance, it is a paper with technical flaws, weak evaluation, inadequate reproducibility, and incompletely addressed ethical considerations.
>
> ...
>
> 20. I acknowledge that I have read the authors' rebuttal and made whatever changes to my review where necessary.
>
> Agreement accepted.
>
> (Adapted from an anonymous real example.)

Project

Work in groups. Ask your supervisors or other students about whether or not they have received an editor decision letter with the reviewers' comments in their own disciplines and then work out a detailed outline of these responses. Prepare a presentation to be delivered in class.

Unit 8

Bio-notes and CVs

Part I
Introducing the Unit

Both bio-notes and CVs in academia are brief accounts providing significant information relevant to the understanding of a person's academic life or activities. For example, when our articles get accepted or when we are preparing a public presentation, we will often be asked for a short academic biography. Or when we apply for academic, education, scientific, or research positions, as well as for fellowship programs and grants, a CV is a tool to help us move from an application to an interview.

It seems simple for us to write these two types of academic biographies, but we will soon get awkward and tricky when we try to show how amazing we are without sounding arrogant or pretentious. For many people, it is more difficult to write these academic bios than dissertations. How do we sum up ourselves and our work in just a few sentences? What do we need to include? What should we leave out? In this unit, we will compare the two types of academic biographies and learn about their wording, formats, and structures.

After finishing this unit, you are expected to achieve the following learning objectives:

- to understand the essential information included in the bio-notes and CVs for academic activities;
- to be acquainted with the differences and similarities between the two types of academic biographies;
- to use signal phrases and typical templates in writing bio-notes and CVs for different purposes.

Unit 8　Bio-notes and CVs

Part II
Learning Useful Expressions

Study the bold-faced expressions that are often used in bio-notes and CVs for academic activities.

A. Stating the Personal Information, Education Background, and Professional Experiences

- Chen Ning Yang, **byname** Frank Yang, (born September 22, 1922, Hefei, Anhui Province, China), is a **Chinese-born American theoretical physicist** who made significant contributions to physics.
- Professor Rebelsky **is currently Vice Chair of** the ACM Special Interest Group on Computers and Society and **Information Director for** the ACM Special Interest Group on Computer Science Education.
- Please find the details of **contact information** in the application package.
- Maria Blair is also **a Ph.D. candidate** at Stanford University.
- Walter Smith's **major research experience includes** the extensive neuropsychological and psychodiagnostic assessment for children.
- She **received her bachelor's degree in** Computer Engineering **from** Escuela Superior Politécnica del Litoral (ESPOL) in Guayaquil, Ecuador.
- She also **holds a M.Sc. in** Computer Science **from** the University of Illinois, Chicago.
- He **obtained her PH.D. in** Computer Science **from** the University of Iowa, **under the direction of** Dr. Ben Lyons at the Learning Technology Group Lab.
- Sanjay Gupta is **a member of** the faculty of the Department of Neurosurgery at the Emory University School of Medicine in Atlanta.
- Sarah Chen **held a teaching position in** the Department of Chemical Engineering from 2014 to 2018.

B. Stating the Academic or Research Interests

- Dr. Ping Zhou's **academic interests include** high-energy astrophysics, interstellar medium, and (pre-)historical transients.
- **His areas of interest and research** include the design of combustion systems and aspects of combustion **ranging from** increasing efficiencies **to** reducing

- pollutant emissions.
- His research **focuses specifically on** the association of sugar intake and calcium loss of human bodies.
- Her research focused on the structure and mechanism of membrane transport proteins, **exemplified by** the glucose transporter GLUT1 and voltage-gated sodium and calcium channels.
- In addition to my research, I have **contributed to** enhancing the success of students through teaching, service, and mentoring.
- Jamie Oliver **is currently working on** magnetooptical trapping of a Lithium-Rubidium species.
- Most of my research **centers on** non-biological stresses such as exposure to foreign compounds, or unfavorable temperatures (heat or chilling).
- Over the last five years, Jaime Bayly **has become involved in** observational projects using big telescopes such as XMM-Newton, IRAM, and LOFAR.
- Prof. Chen Yong's **teaching areas** are supernova remnants and interstellar medium.

C. Stating Honors and Professional Activities

- Dr. Sandra Webster, Westminster College professor of engineering, **made several conferences presentations** during her visit to the College of St. Benedict in St. Joseph, Minnesota.
- Assistant professor of Law Aman Gebru **received a** faculty development **grant of** $10,000 and the Reverend Alphons Loogman Faculty Research Grant of $6,500.
- In August 2016, Catherine Jones **obtained an internship at** the University of Rochester REU Program, Rochester, NY.
- Professor Craig has **authored, co-authored, edited, or co-edited** almost 300 **publications** on high-energy astrophysics.
- Jennifer Phillips has **co-edited a number of books on** X-ray astronomy and **published** over 30 **papers** in 8 journals.
- Ian Hacker **received** the Berkeley Undergraduate **Scholarship** in 2021.
- In 2020, he **received the award for his contribution to** the health sector as well as the vaccine production in the country.
- He **holds the membership of** such academic organizations as ACM, AAUP, and IEEE.

D. Describing Skills and Personalities

- He has clear spoken and written **communication skills**, patience, and **a meticulous attention to details**.
- Rochester **demonstrates a strong power of** analytical reasoning in conducting primary and secondary source research.
- As an **experienced** developer, he **is skilled in** portal development.
- He **is fluent in** both English and German languages.
- He **is proficient in** HTML coding and data analytics.
- He is **punctual**, **hard-working**, and **dedicated with** great initiative and leadership skills.
- She displays her communicative skills and **collaborative capabilities** in the key projects.

Part III
Learning Ways of Organization

In this part, we are going to discuss the similarities and differences between the two types of academic biographies with regard to their contents, formats, and structures.

Writing a Scholarly Bio-note

As the name suggests, a bio-note, instead of expressing the full highs or lows of one's life, is a short verbal description of important facts in an individual's life. It goes with a book chapter, or is requested when we submit a paper to a journal or a conference, or is presented on department or personal websites. An example of a bio-note is the About the Author section of a book or article, where the experience or a short biography of the author can be found. When we read submission guidelines of a journal, which vary a lot, we may find almost all of them require a brief biographical statement (or bio-note).

An academic bio-note usually starts with the very basic information including one's full name, positions or titles, and the institution (the education and/or work experience). All the information should be presented in a prose format in the actual academic biography, not listed. For instance, Zhang Wenhong is the Director of the Internal Medicine Department of the Shanghai Medical College.

Meanwhile, the bio-note is often written in the third person because, in general, the third person sounds more professional than the first person. The writer should avoid using "I" to present himself or herself, as though he or she were reading someone else's biography. The bio-note usually starts with the full name, followed by the other information. For example, Joe Smith is currently a Ph.D. candidate at Nanjing University.

One of the main objectives of a biography is to emphasize the writer's accomplishments so as to provide the readers with an overall idea of the writer's academic background. Therefore, it should show how the writer's academic trajectory, academic interests, and research have developed over time. Essentially like a personal advertisement, it should use key terms concisely and professionally to present the writer's research achievements. For example, if the writer focuses on recent COVID-19 vaccine research, the key terms might include: global pandemic, SARS-CoV-2, virus variants, efficacy and effectiveness, and vaccine.

While writing a bio-note, the writer should take context, audience, and purpose into account. For example, if the bio-note is part of a fellowship application, the applicant's expertise and experience should be highlighted so that the reviewers will see his or her strengths. Or if the writer is submitting a biography for the department website, then prospective graduate students, colleagues within the department, and the undergraduate students in the Teaching Assistant section will read it. In each case, consider the audience to determine what aspects of the career and research should be highlighted. For example, Dr. Sanjay Gupta's bio-note on the website of Everyday Health highlights his authority and reputation in the following way: "Dr. Sanjay Gupta is a practicing neurosurgeon and associate chief of neurosurgery at Grady Memorial Hospital and an assistant professor at Emory University Hospital in Atlanta."

For conferences or social media sites, the bio-note is often short, about 35~50 words, including one's name, positions, department, institution, and research interests. In addition to the above information, a mid-length bio-note of 100~150 words used on a department's website contains degrees held, a brief sentence about the dissertation/master thesis, the recent or ongoing scholarly projects, significant publications, and notable awards and honors. On one's personal professional website, a longer bio-note of around 150~400 words can be broken into more than one paragraph and includes additional information such as how the writer's research interests are situated in a larger field of study and connected to the current hot topics in the discipline, non-academic interests or hobbies, and information about one's background (especially if relevant to the research interests).

The sample below displays the essential information to be included in a bio-note.

> Christopher received his B.A. from Williams College and his M.A. and Ph.D. from University of Chicago.
>
> Christopher's research involves the study of association schemes. This study originally arose in statistics, but has since yielded applications to a wide variety of other fields, including coding theory, knot theory, graph theory, and combinatorial designs. In a recent collaboration (to appear in *Communications in Algebra*), Benjamin Drabkin and Christopher have found a new family of non-commutative association schemes with six elements, one for each Mersenne prime. As another example, Christopher recently completed a paper with his collaborator Paul-Hermann Zieschang to prove an analogue of the Schur-Zassenhaus Theorem for association schemes.
>
> Christopher is also interested in ways in which algebraic notions have applications in the sciences and the humanities—for example, in how music theory can be enriched by the study of group theory, or how one can use representation theory to gain useful insights in the study of chemistry and physics.
>
> (Retrieved from the website of Grinnell College.)

This short bio-note from the faculty website gives a very brief introduction to the professor's education background and focuses on his academic interests in mathematics. Considering the possible visitors to the website, the bio-note highlights the professor's research achievements and his publications. It also describes his contribution to the interdisciplinary studies, catering to the students who will apply to this college.

Since an academic bio-note is often used for very formal and academic purposes, the following should be heeded:

- Avoid using informal language such as slang and colloquial words.
- Avoid using humor, unless it is for sure that the intended audience of the media or platform will appreciate it.
- Do not divulge details beyond the current position. Be professional.
- Avoid providing too much personal information. Keep the bio-note succinct and act professionally.
- Do not be circuitous but state the facts directly.

Writing an Academic CV

CV, short for Curriculum Vitae, a Latin word meaning "course of life", should be a thorough, exhaustive account of professional experiences, honors, and activities. A good CV showcases the writer's skills and professional achievements concisely and effectively. The academic CV is essential to applying to graduate programs, scholarships and fellowships, or teaching, research, and administrative positions in academia.

Academic CVs differ greatly from traditional résumés, marketing tools often limited to a single page, because academic CVs usually include details that may not be found in traditional résumés such as fellowships, relevant publications, conferences attended, and awarded funding relevant to a scholarly professional opportunity. They also tend to be longer than traditional résumés: Two pages may be sufficient for a current undergraduate or graduate's CV, while an experienced professor and researcher may have a CV of quite a few pages. Many professors and instructors make their CVs available on their department's faculty biography pages, and these can illustrate varying approaches to style and organization.

When writing an academic CV, the writer should tailor the sections and the order of these sections to the academic field, and to the position that he or she wants to apply for. The CV checklist below demonstrates what to be included in an academic CV:

- Heading: giving personal and contact information, including one's name, e-mail address, mailing address (only one), and phone number.

- Summary / Personal Statement (an optional section): comprising three or four sentences to highlight one's candidacy or capabilities, including one's interests, goals, as well as the most relevant scholarly experience and skills.
- Education: listing one's academic background, including undergraduate and graduate institutions attended, with the details about the institution, location, degree, and date of graduation. If applicable, include one's dissertation or thesis titles, and their advisors.
- Employment History / Work Experience: listing one's employment history in reverse chronological order, including position details and dates. This section might include multiple parts based on one's field. For example, it might contain such subsections as "Teaching Experience", "Research Experience", "Administrative Experience", as well as any service one has done for the department, such as consulting service and administrative work.
- Publications/Books: including any publications, such as books, book chapters, articles, book reviews, and more. Include all of the information about each publication: the title, journal title, date of publication, and (if applicable) page numbers.
- Conferences/Talks: listing any presentations (including poster presentations) or invited talks that one has given. Also list any conferences or panels that one has organized.
- Fellowships/Grants: listing fellowships and grants, including organization names, titles, dates, and the amount of money awarded for each grant, depending on one's field.
- Honors/Awards: including any awards one has received that are related to one's work.
- Certification and Qualifications: listing and highlighting the type of license, certification or accreditation, and dates received as well as key skills and qualifications relevant to one's research and academic work.
- Professional Affiliations and Memberships: listing professional and academic affiliations or memberships one has been active with within the last five years. Mention if one holds a position on the board of any organization.
- Skills/Interests (an optional section): showing a bit more about relevant skills and interests such as a foreign language and other potentially transferrable skills.
- References: listing academics who can provide a reference for one's research, work, and characters (usually around three references), together with their

names and complete contact information.

Regarding the structure and format of a desirable academic CV, the writer should think about the audience, purpose, and context before drafting an academic CV. It is a good practice to research the institution or department and identify what is the most important to the hiring or reviewing committee, taking into consideration their requirements, mission statements, and values. As an organic tool that adjusts to fit the writer's needs, the academic CV should be customized in terms of the content and the order of the sections. When crafting the academic CV, the writer should remove the sections irrelevant to one's field or experience and try to prioritize the sections by including the most relevant accomplishments and experience. In addition, the writer should be consistent with the required format and make it easy to read. Starting each section with a bold-faced section title is helpful for the reviewers to follow the CV better. Finally, the writer should carefully edit and proofread the CV to make it error-free and to show his or her professionalism and scholarship.

Christopher P. French

Curriculum Vitae

Department of Mathematics and Computer Science, Grinnell College

Noyce Science Center, Grinnell, IA 50112

Personal

Born: April 6, 1973, Norwich, CT

Work: 641-269-4839

Home: 641-236-6253

frenchc@math.grinnell.edu

http://www.math.grinnell.edu/~frenchc

Employment

Professor, Grinnell College	2015–present
Associate Professor, Grinnell College	2009–2015
Associate Professor, Grinnell College	2003–2009

VIGRE Research Assistant Professor, University of
Illinois at Urbana-Champaign   2001–2003

Education

Ph.D.	University of Chicago, Chicago, IL	2001
	Thesis Title: "The Equivariant J-homomorphism"	
	Thesis Advisor: J. P. May	
M.S.	University of Chicago, Chicago, IL	1996
B.A.	Williams College, Williamstown, MA	1995
	Mathematics and Classics, summa cum laude,	
	with highest honors in mathematics,	
	Phi Beta Kappa and Sigma Xi	

Teaching Experience

Professor, Grinnell College   2003–present

Courses taught:

Calculus I, Calculus II, Linear Algebra, Symmetry,

Differential Equations, Differential Geometry, Combinatorics,

Elementary Number Theory, Foundations of Algebra, Foundations of Analysis,

Complex Analysis, Topology, Gauge Field Theory, Lie Algebras, Problem Solving Seminar,

a Tutorial on Cryptography, and two Tutorials on Numbers

VIGRE Research Assistant Professor, UIUC   2001–2003

Courses taught:

Advanced Aspects in Euclidean Geometry, Calculus on Curves and Surfaces,

Multivariable Calculus and Vector Analysis

Lecturer in Mathematics, University of Chicago   1998–2001

Courses taught:

Mathematics for Social and Biological Sciences, Studies in Mathematics, Calculus II, III, Elementary Functions and Calculus I, II, III

College Fellow in Mathematics, University of Chicago   1996–1997

TA for Basic Algebra I, II, III: ran problem sessions, graded homework, held office hours, delivered 10 observed lectures

Undergraduate Research Projects Advised

Mentored Advanced Project   Summer 2017

"Extensions of Projection Association Schemes,"

Russ Haight (Grinnell College)

Mentored Advanced Project   Summer 2017

"Realizing Symmetric Hypergroups of Rank 4,"

Bingyue He (Grinnell College)

Mentored Advanced Project   Summer 2016

"Realizing Hypergroups as Association Schemes,"

Bingyue He, Jun Taek Lee (both Grinnell College)

Honors and Awards

Academic Enterprise Leave for Fall 2011

Harris Fellowship for 2006–2007

Attended conference at the University of Chicago:
"Interactions Between Homotopy Theory and Algebra"   July 25–August 6, 2004
    Selected on a competitive basis. Conference included 2 weeks of lectures by invited speakers.

University of Chicago Physical Sciences Division Teaching Award   2001
    Selected on the basis of student nominations.

University of Chicago Department of Mathematics Graves Prize for Teaching   2000

Service Activities

Department of Mathematics and Statistics, chair	2016–2017
Faculty Organization Committee, science division representative	2016–2017
Faculty Organization Committee, chair	2015–2016
Math and Statistics Student Seminar 2012–2016, organizer	2012–2016
Committee on Academic Standing, subcommittee on Academic Honesty (chair in 2008–2009)	2007–2012

Presentations

Noncommutative association schemes of rank 6 with affine subschemes AMS Fall Western Sectional Meeting, Denver, CO   10/8/2017

Noncommutative association schemes of rank 4 Combinatorics/Algebra Seminar, Iowa State University   4/25/2016

Groups of permutations/hypergroups of relations Pure Mathematics Seminar, University of Texas Rio Grande Valley   1/22/2016

Realizing hypergroups as association schemes AMS Central Fall Sectional Meeting, Chicago, IL   10/4/2015

Schemes for extending the theory of extensions of schemes 8th Slovenian Conference on Graph Theory, Kranjska Gora, Slovenia   6/23/2015

Publications and Preprints

1. "Noncommutative Schemes of Rank 6 with Affine Subschemes"

    Joint work with Paul-Hermann Zieschang (under review)

2. "On the Normal Structure of Non-commutative Association Schemes of Rank 6"

    Joint work with Paul-Hermann Zieschang

    Communications in Algebra. 44 (2016), No. 3, 1143–1170.

3. "On a Class of Non-commutative Imprimitive Association Schemes of Rank 6"

    Joint work with Ben Drabkin

> *Communications in Algebra. 43* (2015), No. 9, 4008–4041.
>
> 4. "A Schur-Zassenhaus Theorem for Association Schemes"
>
> Joint work with Paul-Hermann Zieschang
>
> *Journal of Algebra. 435*(2015), 88–123.
>
> 5. "Functors from Association Schemes"
>
> *Journal of Combinatorial Theory,* Series A. *120* (2013), 1141–1165.
>
> 6. "A New Semidirect Product of Association Schemes"
>
> *Journal of Algebra. 347* (2011), 184–205.
>
> 7. "Hankel Transforms of Linear Combinations of Catalan Numbers"
>
> Joint work with Michael Dougherty*, Benjamin Saderholm*, and Wenyang Qian*.
>
> *Journal of Integer Sequences. 14* (2011), Article 11.5.1.
>
> 8. "The Equivariant J-homomorphism for Finite Groups at Certain Primes"
>
> *Algebraic Geometry and Topology. 9* (2009), 1885–1949.
>
> (Retrieved from the website of Grinnell College.)

  In the CV above, the very first section is the scholar's name and his current employer followed by the very detailed personal information titled "Personal". In the following sections of "Employment" and "Education", the author lists all the previous and current positions as well as his degrees and where he received his education. In the sections of "Teaching Experience" and "Undergraduate Research Projects Advised", he lists all the important courses he has ever taught and the contributions he has made in his teaching positions. In the "Honors and Awards" and "Service Activities" sections, important awards in his career and his principal academic services are enumerated in the time sequence. What takes the largest proportion of this CV is his academic activities including his presentations and publications, displaying his academic achievements and capabilities. All the information in this CV is organized in the reverse chronological order so that the readers can learn about the latest academic activities and performance of this scholar.

  In the global community of researchers, to build a verified record of one's research activities, which is interoperable with all the different publishers, funders, and institutions, a persistent digital identifier called ORCID (short for "Open Researcher and Contributor Identifier") is created to distinguish researchers from one another. Scholars can connect their ORCID iD with their professional information—affiliations, grants, publications, peer review, and more. They can use their ORCID iD to share their information with other systems, ensuring they get recognition for all the contributions, saving their time and hassle, and reducing the risk of errors. The scholars can add a brief biography of no more than 5,000 characters to their ORCID records to provide a narrative description about their research and career interests.

To sum up, different from the traditional résumés in other fields, academic bio-notes and CVs give the essentials of scholars' academic careers and highlight their professional achievements.

Part IV
Analyzing the Examples

In this part, we are going to analyze some examples so as to understand the wording, structures, and moves of bio-notes and CVs for academic activities.

I. **Compare the following two bio-notes and answer the questions.**

Bio-note 1

Jerome Groopman, M.D., is the Dina and Raphael Recanati professor of Medicine at Harvard Medical School, chief of Experimental Medicine at Beth Israel Deaconess Medical Center, and one of the world's leading researchers in cancer and AIDS. He is a staff writer for *The New Yorker* and has written for *The New York Times, The Wall Street Journal, The Washington Post,* and *The New Republic*. He is an author of *The Measure of Our Days* (1997), *Second Opinions* (2000), *Anatomy of Hope* (2004), *How Doctors Think* (2007), and the recently released, *Your Medical Mind.*

(Retrieved from Jerome Groopman's website.)

Bio-note 2

Max Tegmark is a professor of Physics at MIT. His research has ranged from cosmology to the physics of cognitive systems, and is currently focused at the interface between physics, AI, and neuroscience.

A native of Stockholm, Tegmark left Sweden in 1990 after receiving his B.Sc. in Physics from the Royal Institute of Technology (he'd earned a B.A. in Economics the previous year at the Stockholm School of Economics). His first academic venture beyond Scandinavia brought him to California, where he studied physics at the University of California, Berkeley, earning his Ph.D. in 1994.

After four years of West Coast living, Tegmark returned to Europe and accepted an appointment as a research associate with the Max Planck Institute for Physics in Munich. In 1996 he headed back to the U.S. as a Hubble Fellow and member of the Institute for Advanced Study, Princeton. Tegmark remained in New Jersey for a few years until an opportunity arrived to experience the urban northeast with an assistant professorship at the University of Pennsylvania, where he received tenure in 2003. He extended the East Coast experiment and moved north of Philadelphia to the shores of the Charles River (Cambridge-side), arriving at MIT in September 2004. He is married to Meia Chita-Tegmark and has two sons, Philip and Alexander.

Tegmark is an author on more than 200 technical papers, ranging from the physics of cognitive systems to precision cosmology and the ultimate nature of reality, all explored in his popular book *Our Mathematical Universe*. He has featured in dozens of science documentaries and has received numerous awards for his research, including a Packard Fellowship (2001–2006), Cottrell Scholar Award (2002–2007), and an NSF Career grant (2002–2007), and is a Fellow of the American Physical Society. His work with the SDSS collaboration on galaxy clustering shared the first prize in *Science* magazine's "Breakthrough of the Year: 2003".

For more on his research, publications, and students, or his fun articles, goofs, and photo album, please visit Personal home page.

(Retrieved from the website of Massachusetts Institute of Technology.)

Unit 8 Bio-notes and CVs

Questions:

1. Where do you expect to read the two bio-notes respectively? For what purposes?

2. How are the two bio-notes organized respectively?

3. What are the similarities and differences between them?

II. Compare the following two academic CVs and answer the questions.

CV 1

陈开明 (Kai Ming Ting)

Professor, School of Artificial Intelligence

Nanjing University, Xianlin Campus Mailbox 603

E-mail: tingkm@nju.edu.cn

Research Interests

　　Isolation kernel

　　Mass-based similarity

　　Mass estimation and mass-based approaches

　　Ensemble approaches

　　Data stream data mining

　　Machine learning

Short Biography

　　After receiving his Ph.D. from the University of Sydney, Australia, Kai Ming Ting worked at the University of Waikato (NZ), Deakin University, Monash University, and Federation University in Australia. He joined Nanjing University in 2020.

　　Research grants received include those from National Science Foundation of China, U.S. Air Force of Scientific Research (AFOSR/AOARD), Australian Research Council, Toyota InfoTechnology Center, and Australian Institute of Sport.

　　He is one of the inventors of Isolation Forest and Isolation Kernel. Isolation

Forest is widely used in industries and academia. Isolation Kernel is a unique similarity measure which is derived from a dataset based on the same isolation mechanism as Isolation Forest.

Qualifications

Graduate Certificate of Higher Education—Monash University, 2004

Ph.D., Basser Department of Computer Science—University of Sydney, 1996

Master of Computer Science—University of Malaya, 1992

Bachelor of Electrical Engineering—University of Technology Malaysia, 1986

Selected Program Committees

Area Chair: International Joint Conference on Artificial Intelligence, 2021

Program Co-chair: The Twelfth Pacific-Asia Conference on Knowledge Discovery and Data Mining, Osaka, Japan, 2008

Tutorial Co-chair: The Eighth Pacific-Asia Conference on Knowledge Discovery and Data Mining, Sydney, Australia, 2004

Senior PC Member: AAAI Conference on Artificial Intelligence, 2019

Senior PC Member: ACM SIGKDD International Conference on Knowledge Discovery and Data Mining, 2021

Senior PC Member: Pacific Asia Conference on Knowledge Discovery and Data Mining, 2016, 2017, 2021

Program Committee Member (since 2010):

- KDD 2010, 2015–2018: ACM SIGKDD International Conference on Knowledge Discovery and Data Mining
- ICDM 2010–2011, 2014–2016, 2018–2020: IEEE International Conference on Data Mining
- IJCAI 2017: International Joint Conference on Artificial Intelligence
- ECML 2016: European Conference on Machine Learning
- ICML 2010: International Conference on Machine Learning
- PAKDD 2015: Pacific-Asia Conference on Knowledge Discovery and Data Mining

- AISTATS 2021: International Conference on Artificial Intelligence and Statistics

Tutorial Presentation

"Which Anomaly Detector Should I Use?" in 2018 International Conference on Data Mining

"Mass Estimation: Enabling Density-based or Distance-based Algorithms to Do What They Cannot Do" in 2016 Asian Conference on Machine Learning

"Big Data Mining" in Big Data School, 2013 Pacific-Asia Conference on Knowledge Discovery and Data Mining

Software Downloads

Isolation Kernel

Isolation Nearest Neighbor Ensemble

Isolation Forest: A Fast and Effective Anomaly Detector

Mass Estimation and Its Suite of Software

Feating: An Ensemble That Works with SVM

Selected Publications

(Full publication list at http://dblp.uni-trier.de/pers/hd/t/Ting:Kai_Ming)

1. Kai Ming Ting, Jonathan R. Wells, and Takashi Washio (2021). Isolation Kernel: The X factor in efficient and effective large-scale online kernel learning. *Data Mining and Knowledge Discovery*, 35(6), 2282–2312.

2. Ye Zhu, Kai Ming Ting, Mark James Carman, and Maia Angelova (2021). CDF Transform-and-Shift: An effective way to deal with datasets of inhomogeneous cluster densities. *Pattern Recognition,* 117(6191): 107977.

3. Ming Pang, Kai Ming Ting, Peng Zhao, and Zhi-Hua Zhou (2020). Improving deep forest by screening. *IEEE Transactions on Knowledge and Data Engineering*, 1194–1199.

   Doi:10.1109/TKDE.2020.3038799.

4. Jonathan R. Wells, Sunil Aryal, and Kai Ming Ting (2020). Simple supervised dissimilarity measure: Bolstering iForest-induced similarity with class information without learning. *Knowledge and Information Systems, 62*(8): 3203–3216.

5. Sunil Aryal, Kai Ming Ting, Takashi Washio, and Gholamreza Haffari (2020). A comparative study of data-dependent approaches without learning in measuring similarities of data objects. *Data Mining and Knowledge Discovery, 34*: 124–162.

6. Jonathan R. Wells and Kai Ming Ting (2019). A simple efficient density estimator that enables fast systematic search. *Pattern Recognition Letters, 122*: 92–98.

7. Kai Ming Ting, Ye Zhu, Mark James Carman, Yue Zhu, Takashi Washio, and Zhi-Hua Zhou (2019). Lowest probability mass neighbor algorithms: Relaxing the metric constraint in distance-based neighborhood algorithms. *Machine Learning, 108*(2): 331–376.

8. Ye Zhu, Kai Ming Ting, and Mark James Carman (2018). Grouping points by shared subspaces for effective subspace clustering. *Pattern Recognition, 83*: 230–244.

9. Bo Chen, Kai Ming Ting, and Takashi Washio (2018). Local Contrast as an effective means to robust clustering against varying densities. *Machine Learning, 107*: 1621–1645.

10. Yue Zhu, Kai Ming Ting, Zhi-Hua Zhou (2018). Multi-label learning with emerging new labels. *IEEE Transactions on Knowledge and Data Engineering, 30*(10): 1901–1912.

Doi:10.1109/TKDE.2018.2810872.

(Retrieved from the website of Nanjing University.)

> CV 2

CHRIS J. SMITH

424 Elm Avenue, Roanoke VA 01234

631 655 1234 | cjsmith12@gmail.com

EDUCATION

Smith College, Northampton, MA	University of St Andrews, St Andrews, Scotland
Bachelor of Arts, May 2018	Junior Year Abroad, 2016–2017

Major: Physics

Minor: Philosophy

Relevant Astronomy Coursework: Telescopes and Techniques, Introduction to Astronomy, Dark Matter, Nebulae, Extrasolar Planetary Science, Complex Analysis, Nuclei and Particles.

GRANTS AND AWARDS

- Dean's List, 2015–2018
- Fulbright ETA Grant, South Korea, 2018 Finalist
- National Science Foundation Award PHY-0242555, Research Grant, 2018
- Howard Hughes Medical Institution Research Grant (for undergraduate research in the physical sciences), 2017

RESEARCH AND TEACHING EXPERIENCE

- *Research Intern*, University of St Andrews, St Andrews, Scotland, June–August 2017

  Developed optimal process for particle clearing and trapping using optically-mediated Airy beams. Wrote a LabVIEW program with a user-interface that controlled experimental parameters. Conducted experiments using program and analyzed data with MATLAB. Results showed that Airy beams successfully manipulated micro-particles. Procedures will be applied to research involving optical sorting of animal cells and other biological materials.

- *Research Intern*, University of Rochester REU Program, Rochester, NY, June–August 2016

  Researched adaptive optics and orbital angular momentum (OAM) states of light. Set up and performed several experiments to characterize propagation of OAM states through turbulent media. Wrote LabVIEW and MATLAB programs for data collection and analysis. Data suggested that OAM states are good candidates for quantum cryptography.

- *Teaching Assistant*, Smith College Astronomy Department, Northampton, MA, January 2015–May 2018

  Held evening lab hours weekly to assist in teaching laboratory material in introductory astronomy courses. Assisted in solar and night-time telescope observations for Smith faculty, students, and guests.

- *Teaching Assistant,* Smith College Physics Department, Northampton, MA, January 2016–May 2018

  Tutored students weekly in third-year physics course Thermal Physics. Helped students prepare for exams and homework assignments by reviewing concepts in thermal physics, statistical mechanics, and introductory physics. Graded problem sets for General Physics I and II and Modern Physics I.

- *Research Assistant to Dr. Donatella Cassettari*, University of St Andrews, Scotland, October 2016–May 2017

  Participated in a year-long research project that worked towards a future experiment pertaining to magnetooptical trapping of a Lithium-Rubidium species. Wrote Mathematica program to find spontaneous emission rates of a Bose-Einstein condensate system and determined physical parameters for experiment.

- *Research Assistant to Dr. Doreen Weinberger*, Smith College REU Program, Northampton, MA, May–August 2015

  Studied laser diode spectroscopy and saturated absorption spectroscopy of rubidium isotopes. Assembled optical equipment and collected first set of data for use in a future physics laboratory course offered at Smith College.

- *Intern*, Summer Science & Engineering Program (SSEP), Smith College, Northampton, MA, June–August 2015

Assisted in teaching fundamentals of physics and engineering to high school girls for Music and Engineering course offered through SSEP. Oversaw group work and machine shop sessions. Guided students in construction of their end-of-program projects, a musical instrument employing applications of physics and engineering. Organized and led recreational activities after class.

PUBLICATIONS

O'Sullivan-Hale, M. et al. including C. J. Smith. "Propagation of Orbital Angular Momentum States of Light in Turbulent Media" (to be published).

Baumgartl, J. et al. including C. J. Smith. "Particle Clearing and Trapping Using Optically-mediated Airy Beams". *Optical Express* (2018).

PRESENTATIONS

- "Propagation of Orbital Angular Momentum States of Light in Turbulent Media"
- Symposium on Undergraduate Research DLS Meeting LS-XXIV, Rochester NY, October 2017

TECHNICAL SKILLS

JavaScript, MATLAB, Mathematica, LabVIEW, LaTeX, Adobe Illustrator, Adobe Photoshop

ACTIVITIES

Vice President / Treasurer, Smith College Physics Club, October 2016–May 2018

Presented and filed budget forms. Provided guidance and insights for students inquiring about physics degree and physics department. Searched for and advertised physics-related events during the year. Promoted student-faculty camaraderie.

VOLUNTEER WORK

- Habitat for Humanity, Smith College, Northampton, MA, 2015–2017
- Participated in building houses on several sites in Western Massachusetts

(Retrieved from "CV Samples" on the website of Smith College.)

 **Questions:**

1. What are the differences between the two academic CVs?

2. Who do you think might be the writers of the two academic CVs respectively?

3. For what purposes do they write the CVs respectively?

📖 Exercises

I. **Translate the following Chinese sentences into English using the appropriate expressions chosen from the box.**

> - receive/win a(n) award/prize for…
> - receive a grant of…
> - focus on the associations between…and…
> - be elected a member of…
> - major research experience includes…
> - have wide research interests…
> - be known for one's contributions to…
> - have co-edited/co-authored/published…
> - have become involved in…
> - hold the membership of…

(1) 在食品工程领域，Doudna 已经与他人合作出版了 6 本书，独立发表了 30 多篇期刊论文。

_____

_____

(2) 他最近的研究特别关注大气新粒子的形成与环境变量之间的非线性联系。

_____

_____

(3) 2020 年，这两位女科学家因开发了一种被比作"分子剪刀"的基因编辑方法而获得了诺贝尔化学奖，这种方法有望在未来某一天治愈遗传疾病。

_____

_____

(4) 我的研究兴趣广泛，主要包括人工智能、机器学习、数据挖掘、模式识别、进化计算、多媒体检索等，其中机器学习和数据挖掘是我的核心研究领域。

_____

_____

(5) 中国数学家田刚以其在 Kähler 几何、格罗莫夫 - 威腾理论和几何分析等数学领域的贡献而闻名。

_____

_____

II. Give the subheadings in the left column of the table for the information included in each section of an academic CV provided in the right column.

Curriculum Vitae	
Sections	**Information**
(1) _____	Juan Garcia, 210 W. Green St., Champaign, IL (217)555-1234· rstudent@illinois.edu
(2) _____	**Expected Fall 2022,** Doctor of Philosophy in Civil and Environmental Engineering, University of Illinois at Urbana-Champaign, Dissertation title: "Visualizing Geotechnical Engineering Principles" Advisor: Professor Ted S. Visor Juan Garcia, 210 W. Green St., Champaign, IL (217)555-1234· rstudent@illinois.edu
(3) _____	Investigations to improve seismic force-resisting systems through simulations and various visualization techniques.

(Continued)

Sections	Information
(4) _____	**2020–present**, Graduate Research Assistant, Department of Civil Engineering, University of Illinois • Designed and executed small-scale testing to validate control algorithms derived to simulate seismic force-resistance. • Contributed to multi-disciplinary projects aimed at developing visualizations and simulations to predict seismic force damage to various materials. • Collaborated and coordinated with faculty, staff scientists, and fellow graduate students.
(5) _____	**September 2019–present**, Teaching Assistant, Introduction to Structural Engineering College of Engineering, University of Illinois • Prepared lectures and class activities focusing on the analysis of determinate and indeterminate structures for 15–25 freshmen and sophomore-level undergraduates. • Created and graded course assessments to ensure students understand materials and stay on track.
(6) _____	**2021**, Fulbright Scholarship to pursue a Ph.D. • 20 scholarships awarded in Argentina that year **2019**, Flag Honor Guard Member • Qualified by graduating with honors and ranking 4th among engineering majors at UNSJ
(7) _____	**2019–2021**, Carnegie Funding, "The National SMART Grant", $10,000
(8) _____	Garcia, J., Grey, M., and Slater, A. (2020). Evaluation of FEMA 356 Pre-standard for the Seismic Rehabilitation of Buildings. *Journal of Civil Engineering*, Vol.4, No.4, 1231–1268. Doi:10.4236/ojce.2020.64537. Garcia, J. (in press). New Proposal for Seismic Rehabilitation of Hospitals in Argentina. *International Journal of Geoscience*, Vol.2, No.2, 72–98.

(Continued)

Sections	Information
(9) _____	**July 2020**, Facilitator College of Engineering, University of Illinois • Participated in the organization of the Principal's Scholars Program 2020 GEAR UP College Bound Summer Program, where a group of minority children from elementary and middle schools visited the college to learn about different paths in engineering. • Prepared a bridge design competition using popsicle sticks and glue, where the children demonstrated their skills and their creativity.
(10) _____	• English • Spanish • French
(11) _____	**Ted S. Visor**, Professor and Graduate Programs Head Department of Civil Engineering University of Illinois at Urbana-Champaign (217)244-2345, E-mail: tsvisor@illinois.edu **John D. Faculty**, Assistant Professor Department of Civil Engineering University of Illinois at Urbana-Champaign (217)244-1234, E-mail: jdfaculty@illinois.edu **Barbara A. Smith**, Assistant Professor Department of Civil and Environmental Engineering University of Illinois at Urbana-Champaign (217)244-4321, E-mail: basmith@illinois.edu

(Retrieved from "CV Samples" on the website of University of Illinois.)

Unit 8 Bio-notes and CVs

III. **Read the following bio-note and CV and improve them in terms of language use, style, and structure.**

> **Bio-note**
>
> Hi! My name is Cindy. I was originally born in Vermont and now I'm a Ph.D. candidate at North Yankee University in Fargone, New York (in upstate New York). I study emergent medical service. My interest in medical care began as a teenager when I first saw the paramedics saving an old man in the street. I did my undergraduate degree in Biology at SUNY and my master's at UCLA.

> **CV**
>
> **Curriculum Vitae**
>
> **CHEN JUN**
>
> Address: 22, Shenma Road, Nanjing, Jiangsu Province, P. R. China
>
> Tel: 1395647XXX
>
> E-mail: chenXXX@126.com
>
> DoB: January 11, 1995
>
> Nationality: P. R. China
>
> Gender: Male
>
> Martial Status: Single
>
> I am a hard-working student who enjoys working. I am good at cooperating with other students. I have two years of research experience with the professors in environmental science, and I would like to further my studies in a more academic institute.
>
> ACHIEVEMENTS
>
> - 2016 B.S. in Environmental Science, Shanghai University, Shanghai, P. R. China
> - 2018 M.Sc. in Environmental Science, Shanghai University, Shanghai, P. R.

China

EDUCATION

- Major courses include:
    - English: A
    - Mathematics: B
    - Biology: B
    - Chemistry: B
    - Geography: B

RESEARCH INTERESTS AND EXPERIENCE

- Environmental science, particularly soil science
- 2019–2020, Research Assistant, Department of Environmental Science, Shanghai University

HONORS AND AWARDS

- 2020 Top 10 Singers of Shanghai University
- 2019 Third-class People's Scholarship
- 2018 The CBC Bank Scholarship

UNIVERISTY SERVICE

2020, Student Assistant, Office of International Student and Scholar Services, Shanghai University

LANGUAGE

English

IV. Translate the following Chinese bio-note into English using the expressions listed below.

屠呦呦，1930 年 12 月 30 日生于中国宁波，中国著名药学家，中国中医研究院终身研究员兼首席研究员及青蒿素研究开发中心主任。屠呦呦从 1951 年至 1955 年于北京大学医学院药学系学习。毕业之后，屠呦呦在中国中医科学院继续从事中草药研究。

20 世纪 70 年代，经过对传统草药的长期研究，屠呦呦设法从青蒿中提取出一种抑制疟疾寄生虫的物质——青蒿素。从此，基于青蒿素的抗疟药物挽救了数百万人的生命，改善了他们的健康。

Unit 8　Bio-notes and CVs

> 凭借她发现的抗疟新疗法，屠呦呦获得了 2011 年拉斯克临床医学奖，她是第一个获得拉斯克奖的中国人。屠呦呦还获得了 2015 年诺贝尔生理学或医学奖，成为第一位获得诺贝尔生理学或医学奖的中国人，也是第一位获得诺贝尔奖的中国女性。
>
> （改编自"快资讯"网站）

Some expressions that might be used:

青蒿素	artemisinin	疟疾	malaria
抗疟	antimalarial	拉斯克奖	Lasker Award

Project

Work in groups. Suppose you are required to submit a short bio-note and a detailed CV to be posted on an academic website for a self-introduction. Work together as a review committee to peer review the bio-notes and CVs all the group members have drafted and then improve them in terms of language use, style, and structure.

References

杜恬恬，代松，钱滕，朱铭玮，陈丽，张中会，李淑娴．2022．基于核磁共振技术的合欢种子吸水特性．《林业科学》，*58*(4)，22–31.

何香花，张为，庞国防，梁庆华，杨泽，胡才友．2018．帕金森病血尿酸水平的临床研究．中国老年保健医学，*12*(6)，18–21.

李梦涵，陈可江，张卫明，俞能海．2022．基于合成语音的计算安全隐写方法．网络与信息安全学报，*8*(3)，134–141.

栗昕羽，朱梅，李晓乐，程主明，陈雷．2022．远红光辐照对干旱胁迫下生菜种子萌发及幼苗生长的影响．中国农业大学学报，*27*(5)，123–133.

刘玲，陈晓聪，宣焱等．2021．新冠病毒受体蛋白 ACE2 结构与功能的生信分析及原核表达．中国免疫学杂志，1–24.

曾瑜真，杜开锋，金建军等．2022．PI3K 抑制剂联合地塞米松改善氧化应激细胞模型对激素的敏感性及其分子机制．中国免疫学杂志，*37*(12)，1409–1413.

Alley, M. (2018). *The Craft of Scientific Writing*. New York: Springer.

Allien, J. P. B., & Widdowson, H. G. (1974). *English in Focus: English in Physical Science*. Oxford: Oxford University Press.

Ashwinil, K., Saw, G. K., & Singh, A. (2021). Phase-wise spatial and temporal variations of nitrogen dioxide during and pre COVID-19 lockdown period in tier-1 cities of India. *Spatial Information Research*, *29*(6), 887–895.

Azzam, A. Y., Ghozy, S., & Azab, M. A. (2022). Vitamin D and its' role in Parkinson's disease patients with SARS-CoV-2 infection. *Interdisciplinary Neurosurgery*, *27*, 101441.

Bailey, S. (2021). *Academic Writing for University Students*. London: Routledge.

Bartoshuk, L. M., & Klee, H. J. (2013). Better fruits and vegetables through sensory analysis. *Current Biology, 23*(9), R374–R378.

Bellisle, F. (2009). How and why should we study ingestive behaviors in humans? *Food Quality and Preference, 20*(8), 539–544.

Botta, A., Bellincioni, R., & Quaglia, G. (2022). Autonomous detection and ascent of a step for an electric wheelchair. *Mechatronics, 86,* 1–10.

Bottomley, J. (2021). *Academic Writing for International Students of Science.* London: Routledge.

Caffarella, R. S., & Barnett, B. G. (2000). Teaching doctoral students to become scholarly writers: The importance of giving and receiving critiques. *Studies in Higher Education, 25,* 38–52.

Cárdenas, M. L. (2014). Publishing and academic writing: Experiences of authors who have published in PROFILE. *Profiles: Issues in Teachers' Professional Development, 16*(2), 11–20.

Cooley, L., & Lewkowicz, J. (2003). *Dissertation Writing in Practice.* Hong Kong: Hong Kong University Press.

Cotos, E., Huffman, S., & Link, S. (2017). A move/step model for methods sections: Demonstrating rigour and credibility. *English for Specific Purposes, 46,* 90–106.

Davies, A., Veličković, P., Buesing, L. Blackwell, S., Zheng, D., Tomašev, N., Tanburn, R., Battaglia, P., Blundell, C., Juhász, A., Lackenby, M., Williamson, G., Hassabis, D., & Kohli, P. (2021). Advancing mathematics by guiding human intuition with AI. *Nature, 600*(7887), 70–74.

Diao, Y., Wang, J., Yang, F., Wu, W., Zhou, J., & Wu, R. (2021). Identifying optimized on-the-ground priority areas for species conservation in a global biodiversity hotspot. *Journal of Environmental Management, 290,* 112630.

Doroszko, M. (2022). Numerical investigation of the defects effect in additive manufactured Ti-6Al-4V struts on deformation behavior based on microtomographic images. *Materials, 15,* 1–13.

Ekinzog, E. K., Schlerf, M., Kraft, M. Werner, F., Riedel, A., Rock, G., & Mallick, K.

References

(2022). Revisiting crop water stress index based on potato field experiments in Northern Germany. *Agricultural Water Management, 269*, 1–17.

Fan, L., Li, B., Liao, S., Jiang, C., & Fang, L. (2022). High-precision relocation of the aftershock sequence of the January 8, 2022, $M_S6.9$ Menyuan earthquake. *Earthquake Science, 35*(2), 138–145.

Feak, C. B., & Swales, J. M. (2009). *Telling a Research Story: Writing a Literature Review*. Ann Arbor: University of Michigan Press.

Fischer, U., Kaesmacher, J., Strbian, D. Eker, O., Cognard, C., Plattner, P. S., Bütikofer, L., Mordasini, P., Deppeler, S., Pereira, V. M., Albucher, J. F., Darcourt, J., Bourcier, R., Benoit, G., Papagiannaki, C., Ozkul-Wermester, O., Sibolt, G., Tiainen, M., Gory, B., ...Gralla, J.; SWIFT DIRECT Collaborators. (2022). Thrombectomy alone versus intravenous alteplase plus thrombectomy in patients with stroke: An open-label, blinded-outcome, randomized non-inferiority trial. *The Lancet, 400*(10346), 104–115.

Furholt, M. (2021). Mobility and social change: Understanding the European Neolithic Period after the Archaeogenetic Revolution. *Journal of Archaeological Research, 29*, 481–535.

Gao, X., Zhao, J., Zhang, H., Chen, W., & Zhai, Q. (2022). Modulation of gut health using probiotics: The role of probiotic effector molecules. *Journal of Future Foods, 2*(1), 1–12.

Glasman-Deal, H. (2010). *Science Research Writing: A Guide for Non-native Speakers of English*. London: Imperial College Press.

Glendinning, E. (1973). *English in Focus: English in Mechanical Engineering*. Oxford: Oxford University Press.

Horkoff, T. (2015). *Writing for Success*. Victoria: BCcampus Open Education.

Hughes, B. L., Clifton, R. G., Rouse, D. J. Saade, G. R., Dinsmoor, M. J., Reddy, U. M., Pass, R., Allard, D., Mallett, G., Fette, L.M., Gyamfi-Bannerman, C., Varner, M. W., Goodnight, W. H., Tita, A. T. N., Costantine, M. M., Swamy, G. K., Gibbs, R. S., Chien, E. K., Chauhan, S. P., ...Macones, G. A. (2021). A trial of hyperimmune globulin to prevent congenital cytomegalovirus infection. *New England Journal of*

Medicine, 385(5), 436–444.

Ji, S., Xu, W., Yang, M., & Yu, K. (2013). 3D convolutional neural networks for human action recognition. *IEEE Transactions on Pattern Analysis and Machine Intelligence, 35*(1), 221–231.

Klonowska, K., & Bindt, P. (2020, April). The COVID-19 pandemic: Two waves of technological responses in the European Union. Refrieved from Hague Center for Strategic Studies website.

Konnerth, P., Jung, D., Straten, J. W., Raffelt, K., & Kruse, A. (2021). Metal oxide-doped activated carbons from bakery waste and coffee grounds for application in supercapacitors. *Materials Science for Energy Technologies, 4,* 69–80.

Lebrun, J. (2011). *Scientific Writing 2.0: A Reader and Writer's Guide.* Hackensack: World Scientific Publishing.

Li, J., Zhao, Y., Tan, H. S. Guo, Y., Di, C. A., Yu, G., Liu, Y., Lin, M., Lim, S. H., Zhou, Y., Su, H., & Ong, B. S. (2012). A stable solution-processed polymer semiconductor with record high-mobility for printed transistors. *Scientific Reports, 754,* 1–9.

Liu, H., Shao, J., Zhu, G., & Li, Y. (2021). Neoarchean basement, mantle enrichment and crustal extraction in Central Asia: Petrogenesis of 2.5 Ga amphibolite and metadiorite in NE China. *American Journal of Science, 321*(9), 1350–1379.

Maderna, E., & Venturelli, A. (2020). Viscosity solutions and hyperbolic motions: A new PDE method for the *N*-body problem. *Annals of Mathematics, 192*(2), 499–550.

Matthews, J. R., & Matthews, R. W. (2008). *Successful Scientific Writing: A Step-by-step Guide for the Biological and Medical Sciences.* Cambridge: Cambridge University Press.

Merryweather, A. J., Jacquet, Q., Emge, S. P., Schnedermann, C., Rao, A., & Grey, C. P. (2022). Operando monitoring of single-particle kinetic state-of-charge heterogeneities and cracking in high-rate Li-ion anodes. *Nature Material.* https://doi.org/10.1038/s41563-022-01324-z

Mudita, I. M., Cakra, I. G. L. O., Sutama, I. N. S., Mahardika, I. G., & Ariana, I. N. T. (2022). Effectivity of biocatalyst of probiotic lignocellulolytic bacteria as starter of agricultural by-product. *Journal of Biological Sciences, 22,* 11–23.

References

Nejat, M., Manivannan, M., Pericàs, M., & Stenström, P. (2022). Cooperative slack management: Saving energy of multicore processors by trading performance slack between QoS-constrained applications. *ACM Transactions on Architecture and Code Optimization, 19*(2), 21, 1–27.

Paliga, M. (2022). Human-cobot interaction fluency and cobot operators' job performance. The mediating role of work engagement: A survey. *Robotics and Autonomous Systems, 155,* 1–10.

Paquot, M. (2012). *Academic Vocabulary in Learner Writing: From Extraction to Analysis.* London: Continuum.

Patriotta, G. (2017). Crafting papers for publication: Novelty and convention in academic writing. *Journal of Management Studies, 54*(5), 747–759.

Peacock, M. (2002). Communicative moves in the discussion section of research articles. *System, 30,* 479–497.

Peng, Y. J., Lilly, S. J., Kovač, K. Bolzonella, M., Pozzetti, L., Renzini, A., Zamorani, G., Ilbert, O., Knobel, C., Iovino, A., Maier, C., Cucciati, O., Tasca, L., Carollo, C. M., Silverman, J., Kampczyk, P., de Ravel, L., Sanders, D., Scoville, N., ...Scaramella, R. (2010). Mass and environment as drivers of galaxy evolution in SDSS and ZCOSMOS and the origin of the Schechter function. *The Astrophysical Journal, 721*(1), 193.

Ping, H., Wagermaier, W., Horbelt, N. Scoppola, E., Li, C., Werner, P., Fu, Z., & Fratzl, P. (2022). Mineralization generates megapascal contractile stresses in collagen fibrils. *Science, 376*(6589), 188–192.

Russey, W. E., Ebel, H. F., & Bliefert, C. (2006). *How to Write a Successful Science Thesis: The Concise Guide for Students.* Weinheim: Wiley-VCH.

Shen, J., Li, L., Wang, J. P., Li, X., Zhang, D., Ji, J., & Luan, J. Y. (2021). Architectural glazed tiles used in ancient Chinese screen walls (15th–18th century AD): Ceramic technology, decay process and conservation. *Materials, 14*(23), 7146.

Smetana, S., Profeta, A., Voigt, R., Kircher, C., & Heinz, V. (2021). Meat substitution in burgers: Nutritional scoring, sensorial testing, and Life Cycle Assessment. *Future Foods, 4,* 100042.

Swales, J. M., & Feak, C. B. (2012). *Academic Writing for Graduate Students: Essential Tasks and Skills*. Ann Arbor: University of Michigan Press.

The National SARS-CoV-2 Serology Assay Evaluation Group. (2020). Performance characteristics of five immunoassays for SARS-CoV-2: A head-to-head benchmark comparison. *The Lancet, Infectious Disease, 20*(12), 1390–1400.

Wang, L., Zhou, B., Zhao, Z. Yang, L., Zhang, M., Jiang, Y., Li, Y., Zhou, M., Wang, L., Huang, Z., Zhang, X., Zhao, L., Yu, D., Li, C., Ezzati, M., Chen, Z., Wu, J., Ding, G., & Li, X. (2021). Body-mass index and obesity in urban and rural China: Findings from consecutive nationally representative surveys during 2004–2018. *The Lancet, 398*(10294), 53–63.

Wang, P., Wang, H., Chen, W. Q., & Pauliuk, S. (2022). Carbon neutrality needs a circular metal-energy nexus. *Fundamental Research, 2*(3), 392–395.

Wang, X., Lu, X., Li, F., & Yang, G. (2014). Effects of temperature and carbon-nitrogen (C/N) ratio on the performance of anaerobic co-digestion of dairy manure, chicken manure and rice straw: Focusing on ammonia inhibition. *PLOS One, 9*(5), 1–7.

Xu, X., Hall, J., Byles, J., & Shi, Z. (2015). Dietary pattern is associated with obesity in older people in China: Data from China Health and Nutrition Survey (CHNS). *Nutrients, 7*(9), 8170–8188.

Xu, X., Wang, X., Chen, D., Smith, C. M., & Jin, X. (2021). Quantum transport in fractal networks. *Nature Photonics, 15*, 703–710.

Xu, Y., Gui, G., Gacanin, H., & Adachi, F. (2021). A survey on resource allocation for 5G heterogeneous networks: Current research, future trends, and challenges. *IEEE Communications Surveys and Tutorials, 23*(2), 668–695.

Xu, Y., Xiong, B., Chang, Y. C., & Ng., C. Y. (2016). Absolute integral cross sections for the state-selected ion-molecule reaction N_2^+ ($X_2\Sigma_g^+$; $v^+ = 0$–2) + C_2H_2 in the collision energy range of 0.03–10.00 eV. *The Astrophysical Journal, 827*(1), 17.

Yang, J., Zhang, D., Frangi, A. F., & Yang, J. (2004). Two-dimensional PCA: A new approach to appearance-based face representation and recognition. *IEEE Transactions on Pattern Analysis and Machine Intelligence, 26*(1), 131–137.

References

Zhang, H., Ni, W., Li, J., Jiang, Y., Liu, K., & Ma, Z. (2019). On standardization of basic datasets of electronic medical records in traditional Chinese medicine. *Computer Methods and Programs in Biomedicine, 174*, 65–70.

Zhang, L., Zhang, F., Yang, X. Long, G., Wu, Y., Zhang, T., Leng, K., Huang, Y., Ma, Y., Yu, A., & Chen, Y. (2013). Porous 3D graphene-based bulk materials with exceptional high surface area and excellent conductivity for supercapacitors. *Scientific Reports, 3*(1), 1–9.

Zhang, T., Xia, J. Wu, G., & Zhai, J. (2014). Automatic navigation path detection method for tillage machines working on high crop stubble fields based on machine vision. *International Journal of Agriculture and Biological Engineering, 7*(4), 29–37.

Zhao, C., Zheng, Q., & Zhao, J. (2022). Excited electron and spin dynamics in topological insulator: A perspective from ab initio non-adiabatic molecular dynamics. *Fundamental Research, 2*(4), 506–510.

Zhao, J., Cao, Y., Yu, L., Liu, X., Yang, R., & Gong, P. (2022). Future global conflict risk hotspots between biodiversity conservation and food security: 10 countries and 7 Biodiversity Hotspots. *Global Ecology and Conservation, 34*, e02036.

Zheng, Z., Aghili, S. M., &Wüthrich, R. 2022. Towards electroforming of copper net-shape parts on fused deposition modeling (FDM) printed mandrels. *The International Journal of Advanced Manufacturing Technology*, 1–13.

Ziena, H. M., & Ziena, A. H. M. (2022). Nutritious novel snacks from some of cereals, legumes and skimmed milk powder. *Applied Food Research, 2*(1), 100092.